Norman Ten Hundred

Norman Ten Hundred

The 1st (Service) Battalion
Royal Guernsey Light Infantry
in the Great War

A. Stanley Blicq

LEONAUR

Norman Ten Hundred: the 1st (Service) Battalion
Royal Guernsey Light Infantry in the Great War
by A. Stanley Blicq

Leonaur is an imprint of Oakpast Ltd

Material original to this edition and
presentation of text in this form
copyright © 2010 Oakpast Ltd

ISBN: 978-0-85706-373-1 (hardcover)
ISBN: 978-0-85706-374-8 (softcover)

http://www.leonaur.com

Publisher's Notes

The views expressed in this book are not necessarily
those of the publisher.

Contents

This modest work is dedicated to:

Mrs. P. Ereaux

in appreciation of her genial personality, strong moral courage
and unhesitating adherence to duty as she conceived it.

And also to:

George W. Clarke, Esq.

in memory of those Great Days when we marched the
Long Trail together; shared the same sorrows, the same
mirth;—and now the same memories, far away,
indistinct; laughter merged with the tears.

A. Stanley Blicq
Guernsey, 1920

Norman Ten Hundred

A BATTALION OF THE OLDEST AND SMALLEST
DEMOCRACY IN THE WORLD

Guernsey—named Sarnia by the Romans—one of the Channel Isles from out the sun swathed romance of whose shores rallied a fierce band of Norman warriors to the aid of their Duke, William of Normandy; afterwards the Conqueror, at Hastings, 1066. In reward for their valour William granted the Isles the independence they maintain to this day. From Guernsey something approaching 7,000 men have gone out into the Great Undertaking. The Norman Ten Hundred is the 1st Royal Guernsey Light Infantry offered by the States of Guernsey for active participation side by side with the Mother Country's troops in any of the fighting areas. The narrative is authentic.

CHAPTER 1

September–October, 1917

Fed up! Every man of the Ten Hundred was fed up. Thirty-six hours cooped in cattle trucks, thirty or forty in a truck and inhaling an atmosphere that would have disgusted a pig—enough to feed anyone up.

The Belgian frontier was crossed at sunset and the fringe of war's devastation penetrated. Little interest or casual comment was aroused, although a reputable thirsty one remarked that he thought Jerry might have spared the village pub.

The long line of dirty trucks stopped with an abrupt jerk and noisy jarring of impact. Then it came! Grumbles ceased as if by common consent. There was something indefinable but pregnant, and in tense silence ears were strained intently. Was it only the rumble of a distant cart on hard cobbles or...? Faintly over the damp air came a long, insistent murmur. Hearts beat faster.... Guns!

Northward and then West the train panted up a slight grade, made a wide curve and then abruptly shut off steam. Long white tapering lights sprang up from nowhere, wavered and hesitated over the sky; caught in their glare a silvery bird and followed it across the night. Without warning an anti-aircraft gun launched with a deafening roar its whining shell heavenwards. Boom! In the sudden uproar Le Page fell off the train, jerking his tin of bully beef into Clarke's shaving water. The Jerry airman circled higher, dived again—and dropped his bomb, missing the train by hundreds of yards. He had spotted the smoke belching from the engine. Again he spiralled higher, slipped the converging net of searchlights and escaped ... ugh! The Ten Hundred breathed a sigh of relief.

Disembarkation from a train at a point a few miles in the rear of the Front Line always tends to put the wind up you. The mental

11

survey of a thousand men *en bloc* conveys immediately to the mind what an obvious and unmistakable target a battalion forms. Eyes apprehensively search the sky for the danger that each one knows lurks somewhere up there in that black pall, the darker by contrast with the brilliant spearheads of light searching to and fro.

And of course in such windy moments the order to march off is delayed. Then when you *are* well on your way you wish you were not, for there is an unutterable weariness in those marches to bivouacs amid dead silence from end to end of the ranks; only ever present on the ear that unceasing booming of heavies or the nearer and unpleasant *kr-ru-up* of a not-far-distant German shell. Worn, sadly worn, beneath the staggering weight of packs on aching shoulders, where chafed skin smarts under the straps, head bent forward and downwards, one cared little for direction. Onward, always onward, feet burning with heavy going in clogging Belgian mud.... Sleep, one longs to lie down there and then to sleep, anyhow, anywhere!

Bivouacs are under the best of circumstances mere makeshifts. "Stoke Camp"—*Camp!* The irony of it—was on a par with the average. Here and there a scattered tent, here and there a sheet or two of oilcloth, and everywhere an abundance of water.

Still it was a haven of rest. Men filed tiredly by in Companies, sorted themselves out, and cast down packs; boots were jerked off anyhow, rifles stacked. Each man wrapped around him that old and trusty friend—his overcoat, heads rested on the hard packs ... doze and dream....

Three headquarters scouts are turned out for guard!

Two hours swinging up and down, then four hours sleep: and then ... the mind of the overworn first sentry sickens. Again and again over the muddy uneven strip, watching fascinated the weird, mad shadows cast in gaunt trees from a perpetual red glow eastwards. From amid the bivouacs a lad cries fitfully in his uneasy sleep; a hardy few can be seen by the glow of cigarettes sitting beneath a solitary tarpaulin.

From the distance something high in the heavens hummed softly the while here and there far-off searchlights twinkled, one after another picking up the trail until the whole sky was ablaze with wavering shafts of light. The murmuring grew to a roar, accompanied by a deafening din of an Archie (anti-aircraft) barrage and the unceasing rattle of machine guns.

The enemy 'plane became visible, its sinister cross plainly discernible, and dived. The sentry heard something sizzle down and—a mighty flash lit up the woods: the whole earth trembled violently beneath a fierce concussion. The roar echoed and re-echoed, was followed by a continuous shower of litter tearing or trickling down through the trees. Unnerving cries rose from a score or more stampeding horses in the adjacent camp; but the subtler human ear caught on the damp night breezes a sound that froze the blood ... pitiful low sobs of men dying from the hot flying shrapnel.

The Guernseys slept on as if nothing had happened. Therein lies the strange psychological mystery of the human mind.... The bomb failed to disturb; but a solitary shot from the sentry would have roused half the Battalion and sent them seeking half-consciously for their rifles.

In the morning the news spread rapidly. In it they found occasion to accentuate a grousing born of the damp, uncheering vista around them.

"Bombed in the train, bombed first night up 'ere," said Ginger, "grub late, no water to wash in; no baccy, no matches—only a blasted ole rifle wot's gone too rusty to clean."

Washing WAS a complex problem, involving choice between half-a-mile's walk to a doubtful pool or a canteen full (about a pint and a half) of water obtained from a muddy puddle in the roadway. The latter method requiring a minimum of physical exertion was by far the more popular and each tin of valued water underwent utilisation to its very extreme limits, i.e., until reduced to something approaching a soup.

There are always days when the Ten Hundred arouse within themselves by their own exertions a shy, deep pride of their Regiment. It is a characteristic happy knack of the boys to give their very best during parades before the G.O.C., and that was undoubtedly a strong factor in building up the Battalion's fame at Bourne Park.

They visibly and agreeably impressed the G.O.C., 29th Division, at their initial appearance before him. Whether the Guernsey's exceptional steadiness solicits approval, or if the rapid rhythmical movements in handling arms—quicker than is customary with other regiments—pleases the Official Eye cannot be accurately gauged. It is a concrete certainty, however, that the unit composes an efficient, compact body comparing very favourably with its contemporaries.

Fritz carried on his genial bombing expeditions night and day over the surrounding district, thereby giving birth to defensive measures in the form of an excavation inside each tent two feet in depth. Outside a wall of similar height was constructed around the tent or bivouac—few have the luxury of a tent. A degree of protection from flying shrapnel is thereby obtained, unless, of course, Fritz registers a direct hit.

Miniature dug-out were cut down into the wet soil by the more enterprising, but proved ghastly failures, even in the dry hours ... if anything out there could be termed "dry." I doubt it, excepting the thirst of a few reputables. Twenty-four hours' rain gave the most ambitious dug-out an opportunity to demonstrate its exceptional capability of receiving and *retaining* water. The scene presented in the morning was unique. A steel helmet sailed majestically behind an empty tin of bully, in turn twirling by a pair of sunken boots. Clinging desperately to a few wet sandbags, four marooned muddy individuals glared ferociously at the interested onlookers and developed fearful vocal powers of emphasis that shocked the genial enquirers who came in dozens to discover if: "A rain-drop or two had trickled in."

The peculiarity of being bombed is such that a sense of personal security takes a long while to outlive the insistent curiosity that compels one to stare fascinated at the death above. An up-stretched neck and straddle-legged attitude predominated—so did neck-ache.

White, during a raid, threw a stone upon Tubby's hat, causing the latter to drop his mess-tin of dinner in hasty fright ... but the sight of the stew sliding gracefully down White's blankets delighted the onlookers and made "honours easy."

The Ten Hundred, of course, attempted to bring a Jerry down. Sergeant Russel nightly pointed the muzzle of his Lewis-gun in the air and pulled the trigger, in the hope perhaps that Fritz might inadvertently sail into the track of his bullets. Unfortunately firing at so perpendicular an angle caused the lead to fall into the adjacent infantry lines and they—they returned the compliment, although neither Battalion inflicted any "Blighty's" on the other.

Two Companies had to go up the line on a hazardous task. The twist of the coin gave the honour to A. and D. And yet how forcible a factor was that coin in deciding the unfathomable wherefore of existence. It was thrown in the air; fell, wavered on edge, flattened out. And implicitly, blindly obeying the indict conveyed from its face this or that man passed from active, living phenomenon in the evolution of the cosmic process to mere insensible matter.

Life, then, is chance, luck; to which no guiding factors, laws, or binding principles can be adduced.

Before marching off from the bemudded "parade" ground we were fed up. Constant rain had rendered an always muddy surface into a slimy quagmire, in which every step forward was a conscious effort. There was little singing in either Companies (A. and D.), during the short march to the train conveying the party to near a shell-infested area where the said party would partake of its outdoor picnic. "Party"—the ironical humour of it!

Each lad was tired, wet, and hungry. Tempers easily ruffled. "Wot the 'ell do yer think year bumpin' into?" shouted Biffer at an unfortunate who had side-slipped into him.

"Bumpin' into?" the other grunted, "nothing much by the look of it." They glared at one another like fighting cats ... the contretemps fizzled out; both were too tired to argue.

Disembarkation during the night in a blinding storm of rain that had materially increased to a torrential downpour materially helped to damp spirits already none too high. Bumping wildly into this figure or that, slipping full-length into inches of water and thereby saturating what little dry clothing that had remained so, they peered vainly into the all absorbing blanket of night for the tents, bivouacs or shelters that were not there. We have all had our minds permeated with a strong fear of Hell.... After that night many will thank their stars that this abode of ill-omen is *hot* and therefore apparently *dry*.

Each man was told to do the best for himself with a ground sheet. To derive shelter in such a storm with a few feet of oilcloth, no props, no light, is a task to which sweeping back the Atlantic with a toothbrush is simple in comparison.

But they were up against it ... grumbles ceased. Someone by an extraordinary stroke of luck stumbled upon an R.E. dump from which sundry articles essential to the construction of shelters could be filched. Filched must be emphasised, for therein lay the ulterior reason for transformation from "fedupity" to a genial anticipation of forthcoming trouble. The C.R.E. in the morning would raise Hell when he discovered half his dump appropriated and scattered by the Guernseys over a wide area. The O.C.'s of A and D Companies would be hauled over the coals.... There was the nucleus of the farce. The men pinched and the officers stood the racket. The very thought sent the whole ranks chuckling and up soared the high spirit barometer. There was, too, in these repeated silent visits to the dump a possibility of discovery that appealed to that venturesome spirit so characteristically a trait of the Ten Hundred. They chuckled gleefully at each nefarious trip, almost wished some interfering N.C.O. would appear from an R.E. depot and originate by his unpleasantries something of a rough house.

Shelters through which streams trickled were run up and the floors tiled with a queer assortment of tins, empty cartridge cases and odd bits of wood. Drenched to the very skin, shivering and sneezing with cold, they gave no heed to the rain tattooing on their faces or to the enemy shells. Within the rickety shelters damp figures, huddled together for warmth, closed tired eyes and in utter weariness of limbs fell into a fitful sleep.

Snatches of song, bursts of laughter, echoed here and there in the night. Laughter! What on earth was there to laugh at? The wretched improvised shelters on and into which rain crept, lashed earthwards by a howling wind? The cold, chilly feet, clinging clothes and wet skin? Or is there anything refreshingly humorous in the knowledge that Death groped about in the night for his own ... found them? Is there a mirth-provoking element in the ten to one chance that *you* may not see the morrow?

All honour to you, Normans! From Valhalla, in his high seat with the Anses, Rollo of old looked down on you with pride.

Langemarck, grim, windswept and desolate.

A few short weeks before it had by the flowing of British blood, by our own Division, been wrenched from the German grasp. There is everywhere about it an awesome sacredness. One hesitates to treat lightly over the soil that belongs to those whose eyes were closed in the taking, and whose warrior forms lie at rest beneath the pathetic white crosses dotted over the gruesome waste. Those sad little emblems of Supreme Sacrifice: "To the memory of a British Soldier." Simple but magnificent! A farewell to some unknown—to some mother's son.

The first shell that scatters you in all direction, secretly feeling yourself doubtfully all over, abruptly disperses any sentimentality that may cling to the mind. The two Companies found it so when they marched still further up the line and commenced work on two different sectors, shelled—but comparatively lightly—for the first day or two.

The first line over-attacked in the mud, swept over Poelcapelle and advanced on Passchendaele, pausing while the mobile artillery moved up to support over roads that were daily filled in and rebuilt by fatigue parties similar to the Guernseys. The German Headquarters concentrated their guns upon the immediate British rear, with the intention of hampering and impeding the movements of rein-forcements and artillery. The Guernseys got the cream of it. Ground was churned up for yards and bodies buried weeks before were blown from their resting places, grinning white and hideous at the sky. Work on the roads was one perpetually interrupted operation, men ducking every few minutes to the whine of a shell. Life was an unknown quan-tity—no man could gauge what moments were still left him. Streams of wounded ran, hobbled or limped painfully away from that sector of Hell. Artillery galloped steaming horses through, sighing with relief upon attaining the other end.

There comes a time after his first baptism of fire, after his first view of the shattered mutilated remnants of a shell-stricken body, that the infantryman turns towards where invisible German guns from com-parative safety belch forth death, and shakes his impotent fist at this enemy. He picks himself up, white and shaken, from where the con-cussion has thrown him, and amid the cries of the dying, "Curse you," he sobs, "if ever the chance comes—!"

A battery of R.F.A. within a few hundred yards of the road opened salvoes lasting throughout every morning until the ears throbbed with each successive roar and the earth trembled violently beneath the 6-in.'s concussion. Jerry airmen endeavouring to spot the gun-po-sitions swooped down unheard, pumping lead in heavy showers from machine-guns upon the Guernseys and scattering them broadcast.

Pike stopped a "Blighty" with his foot, and Pleton, a shrapnel bul-let whistling clean through his chest, fell limply forward. Gas com-menced, coming over in shells ... in response to the alarm, respirators were donned with an alacrity phenomenal in its hasty adjustment. De La Mare discovered one of the eye-pieces missing. Holding his nose with one hand, he spluttered: "Wa', wi' I do?" and instantly clapped his hand over his mouth, jumping from one foot to another in apprehen-sive uncertainty. From within every helmet choking bursts of laughter sounded muffled on the air. The unfortunate lad held his breath until black in the face, gasped in a frenzied intake of air, and gingerly felt himself. Ultimately instructed to change into the P.H. helmet, he did so nervously, succeeded, and sat down, inhaling deep breaths of relief.

"All Clear" was sounded, but from the moment he removed his mask and for days afterwards he was the recipient of sly solicitations from a chuckling platoon.

"I wonder why 'e was pullin' on 'is nose?" Le Page innocently inquired; "ain't it long enough?"

"Dunno," Ginger replied; "p'raps 'e 'as chronic catarrh!"

Day followed day, bringing little change in the task. Casualties were not exceptionally heavy, but the strenuous work and perpetual stress of the nerves told on them. For there is no more nerve-shattering task than to have to submit without active retaliation day after day to harassing shell-fire. It is during this early initiating into a general expectation of possible death that the young warrior has to conquer the psychological instinct impressed with fear upon his imagination from childhood that *life* is his most valued asset, and must be safeguarded before all things. And now his conception is revolutionised. He must accept death as a daily possibility.

It is patent that dusk found them weary and worn, plodding and wading silently "homewards," shovel on shoulder, across four or five kilos of desolate mud; falling and tripping over stagnant bodies, masses of tangled wire, bricks and jagged wood-work everywhere impeding progress. And yet a consciousness of good work done reacted on their spirits. They reflected contentedly of the meal awaiting, of their pipes, their sleep.

The inscrutable ways of Chance—Destiny, call it what you will—brought about the greatest catastrophe that had so far obtained in the Guernsey ranks. Major Davey moved his party over an area—at about 11 in the morning of a warm, sunny Sunday—coming in for a spell of shelling extraordinary in intensity. A labour unit retired because of the exigencies of the precarious situation. Inflexible, the Normans carried on, then—*s-i-iz-z ... kr-rupp!*

The leading platoon caught it in their very midst, a ghastly heap of mangled flesh and shattered limbs were scattered to right and left. Two unhappy lads were blown to unrecognisable fragments. No words can convey the heart-rending cries of those whose bodies cringe and writhe from the hell-hot agony of searing shrapnel. There is an unmistakable appeal for pity that stirs the depth of feeling until a wild frenzy to right matters sends Berserk passion to the brain. Oh, you German gunners in your serene safety, if ever my chance comes...!

Thus the first of the Ten Hundred went over the Great Divide.

An order to retire was quietly obeyed. They marched back, some shaken, some bleeding from minor wounds: bearing the stretcher cases and dead with them. Some gazed eastwards, faces transfigured with impotent rage, a few white faced boys stared hypnotised before them; but the remainder, heads erect, looked grimly ahead ... they would not forget!

A day or so later the Normans came out. Cookie, black and grimy from head to foot—the only condition in which he really felt at home—prepared the removal of his cookers.

"I didn't 'alf 'ave the wind up," he confided me afterwards, "about that there last dinner; becos, you see, a Jerry shell wot burst close chucked a great chunk of mud into one of them cockers. Wot was I to do? Couldn't throw away the grub ... didn't 'ave no more, so I just stirred it all up. Anyhow," reflectively, "it made it thicker, and they sez it was 'tray bun.'"

And so they came away with out farewell glance across that tragic countryside, lonely and desolate as if God-forsaken in its very devastation. The eye took in the reflected light in a myriad pools, the white crosses, sinister wire trekking right away to where a few solitary tree stumps stood up madly against the skyline. They thought with a pang of those who slept the long last sleep in the clinging wet soil, whose footsteps would no longer ring on the hard road in rhythmic chorus with the old Ten Hundred, whose voices would ne'er again swell the Battalion's marching rallies....

Following a brief rest the 29th Division trained, from Poperinghe southwards. The same weary cooping in cattle-trucks, same monotonous crawl. And yet during a halt at Hazebrucke arose one of those moments that live long in memory, when patriotism rises high in the breast. The station was crowded with soldiers and civilians as the Guernseys' train drew up in the cool, dusky evening light. Someone played a cornet: "The long, long trail." From end to end of the train the Ten Hundred caught it up and sang low in their soft southern accent. A hush fell on the chattering onlookers, they turned and stared. The harmony enveloped them, stirred them ... and we, ah, how the blood stirs even now. But the memory saddens—for the voices of many are for ever still.

CHAPTER 2

September–October, 1917
—Hendecourt

The mad rattle of strife in Belgium had throbbed on the ear-drums incessantly day and night, but on the frontage beyond Hendecourt and Arras little more than an occasional "Verey" light from the Fritz line played hesitatingly on the grotesque landscape. Even the guns were silent: the crack of a rifle-shot or far-off splutters from machine-guns were the only sounds to mingle with the harsh jumbled tread of the Royal Guernseys marching over cobbles and bad roads to the encampment of iron huts.

The going from Beaumetz, through shell-shattered villages, by roads twisting up and down long hills, commenced to tell on the men long before the first halt was due. Breathing became, in many cases, long and heavy; some stumbled blindly forward with heads strained down, and others impotently cursed at the Higher Command for not calling a halt. Sweat trickled over dust-begrimed countenances, feet were aching, the tongue clove parched to the mouth, the pack ... oh, the utter hell of it. And yet on the morrow you forgot!

On territory recaptured (during March, 1917) from Fritz and within a few hundred yards of his original reserve line, still intact and heavily protected with barbed wire, was the conglomeration of huts that formed for nearly three weeks the home of the Ten Hundred.

The Infantryman sees far more of the trenches than of Rest Camps, and therefore what precious days of absence from the joys of water-logged dug-outs comes his way are seized upon and lived to the very full. The Normans had not experienced very much—but they had had quite enough. Ginger Le Ray, basking his fair unshaven features in the sun and lovingly watching Lomar pulling at a fat (and dubious) cigar, aired the Battalion's sentiments with: "This is orlright. Anything except Paschendaele or my ole woman."

A Battalion offers widely divergent contrasts in the psychology of men composing its ranks, and it is with the intention of bringing the reader into intimate and personal touch with all these types of men that this chapter is penned. Nick names are as common as daisies in the Army and by this medium a large number of characters will be portrayed and the fate awaiting each one later recorded. To those who imagine that Death has set laws for claiming this or that type there will be ample argumentative data—but this is a factor upon which no scientific grounds can be used as a base for theories. Life is chance!

There are good, indifferent, and bad soldiers among the Normans. The first can be disposed of briefly: They are never adrift, never for Company Orders, always spotless and first on parade; perpetually shining and exhibiting glistening buttons before the Company-Sergeant-Major in vague hope of promotion. A detestable type, fortunately in the minority. Of "indifferent" in the above sense but inordinately proud of their Battalion on parade and who gave of their best when demanded, 80 per cent. of the Norman element was formed.

And the bad! Dare devils and schemers of the deepest dye, ever on the *qui vive* to dodge fatigues, caring not a brass button for the C.O. himself. Martel, Leman, White, Evans. Good fellows all. Afraid of nothing except hard work, shining-up and guards. Nebo, whose ankle when its owner was nabbed for a working party, would twist beneath him and features twisted in pain would murmur: "Can't—can't carry on." The Duo (Blicq and Clarke), imperturbable and calm, had strong aversion to exertion in any form. The appearance of a N.C.O. requiring "Four men for fatigue." sent the two flying headlong for the doorway with a great show of towels and soap. Always in trouble, they always wriggled out. Stumpy, also, too tired to slip away, too tired to be anything but a hindrance when they did put him on a job, but never too weary to eat a dinner not his own. But to them all, good, indifferent or bad, the Battalion's name and record came *first*. To no unit, however famed, would they acknowledge superiority and every General who reviewed them was unable to repress appreciation of the outcome of this latent *esprit de corps*.

They tackled every Regiment in the Brigade at football and defeated one and all, fought their way by sheer tenacity into the Brigade Cup Final—and lost with good spirit.

Parades were few and light, sport compulsory. Moral and health

21

were excellent although the genial company of the leech-like post of active service—lice—began to irritate some few and to send creepy sensations down the spine of those who were still unblessed. The Duo scrubbed each other daily in—a biscuit tin of water.

There were baths of course! You marched down in twenties to where a "room" was screened from the eyes of those who were not there to see by a bordering of sacking—this served also to "keep out" a shrieking cold wind that played up and down your bare body with icy persistence, and finally with a spiteful gust whisked away your solitary towel to the skies and caused you to ponder how Adam warmed himself in a snowstorm. To pass from this elaborate dressing-room to the actual torture-chamber necessitated a short walk *outside—ugh!* Once inside the twenty Spartans waited for the water to be turned on them from the long spray pipes. Sometimes this water froze your marrow, but generally it scorched away the hair that should have been shaved off that morning. However, splashing and blindly soaping each other you would be half-way through the operations when steam was shut off with the order "clear out"—to make way for another twenty animals. Thus, eyes clenched tight to omit soap-suds, into the open again, a slip in the mud, and, forgetting, abrupt opening of the eyes—how wonderfully expressive and voluminous is our English tongue. Although I have heard a no more efficient flow of useful blasphemy than Duport's vitriolic patois.

Rations were certainly plentiful—with the exception of bread, of which one man's issue would not choke a winkle.

Breakfast was usually bacon or cheese and *chah* (tea)—the beverage slightly tainted with sugar; although there is on record one memorable occasion of exceptional sweetness of the drink—attributed to the fact that cookie was startled by the shout of "Raid on," and in went the whole bag—minus the quarter placed inside for himse—er, emergency.

Dinner, today, stew. Tomorrow, stew, and the day after—stew! An awful white concoction called rice went with it. Tea finds jam on the menu—on your clothes too, because of a struggle with someone over disputed possession of a pot that did not rightly belong to either. A 1 lb. jar is shared among six—when it is not sixteen. Quantity and quality differ frequently. The variety (Apple and Plum) *never*. Supper, rice. Less said....

Hendecourt proved a posh camp; memories of it and of the men who laughed the heavy days away are pleasant. The Army, despite the

22

grousings that rise steadily to Tommy's lips, is a fine institution, and those who have emerged safely from the Great Undertaking cannot but look back with regretful pleasure upon those great days of the open, of *bonne* camaraderie, of willing sacrifice.

Nightly the 29th Divisional troupe performed before an over-crowded house of the most appreciative audience in the world. A cinema also threw its ardent cowboy lovers and pig-tailed heroines upon a screen whose far distant days may have been spotless and white. Tubby awaited outside the "stage-door" for an hour to interview Tootsie (of the Troupe) after the first night and found "she" wore Army boots, trousers, and chewed plug.

Old theatre house of memory! There on Sunday row on row of mute khaki forms bowed together in unspoken player or sang with quiet, earnest harmony the hymn that tells home every time on the rough warriors' heart: *Holy Father, in Thy keeping ... hear our anxious prayer*, etc. God, how they sang it! Some knew, perhaps, what awaited.

The short November days sent the mud-clogged lads into their huts with the last pale glimmer of a weakly sun. Constructed of sloping corrugated iron, in which no outlet for fire-smoke had been cut, these huts were lined at the top with some substance of felt and through which the rain trickled into puddles and miniature lakes on the ground floor. Clarke had adjusted a tin like a sword of Damocles over his bed to catch the drops—and it certainly conveyed, after falling twice when full upon Stumpy, an apprehension akin to that wrought by the weapon. Over one of these puddles near—*too* near—his bed Ginger was wont to sit with melancholy mien, a rifle held out before him and from the muzzle a string hanging over the water with a mess-tin attached.

"Wot's doin', Gin?"

"Fishin'."

"What for?"

"Me ticket!" (Discharge).

Braziers were rampant in every Company, swelling and overflowing throughout the entire hutments in belching clouds of noxious smoke that permeated an atmosphere impenetrable by human eyes with an odour of smouldering wood, empty milk-tins and tobacco. Those nights!

Those nights of song and laughter, of anticipations, hope, and the yearning for *life*: of long-drawn-out confabs over the glowing embers of a red-hot brazier, the crimson glow shining upon faces that showed so little of aches, fears, longings, masked behind the curling smoke from screening pipes. Silence fall oft-times upon the khaki figures clustered round the genial warmth. Each man to his own dire thoughts ... home, wife, or girl.

Tucked within blankets, heads propped on hands, pipes and cigarettes going, they peered with unseeing eyes into the mad crackle of burning timber. Softly would the melody of a song be hummed, caught up by chorus and wafted out into the indigo mystery of the night. Quiet for a few minutes, an occasional snore and then sure as fate a last parting shot from the Duo.

No. 1: "No one knows."

No. 2: "No—and the impossibility—"

No. 1: "Yes. Yet they must. If not, how do they exist?"

Pause and a soft chuckle.

No. 2: "Of course they have. Yet the agony—."

Curiosity overcoming the remainder a series of questions popped up. "What is impossible?", "Why must who?", "What agony?"

No. 1: "You see, no one knows?"

Exasperated chorus: "Knows what?"

No. 1: "Why, if flies have toothache."

And then oblivion claims into its own soundless peace the outstretched forms of rough warriors and removes them from grim reality into the passing realms of a fantastic dream—Arcadia.

Mail days are pleasant. Excited anticipation for your name as each parcel or letter is read out, dull disappointment if your issue is napoo.

Parcels. Oxo cubes, of course. Utilised because of adhesive qualities for throwing at a target as darts. *Café au lait*, a useful preparation for spreading on bread in *lieu* of posie (jam) that has mysteriously evaporated. A pair of silk socks, purple with gold spots. Will come in useful as a rifle rag. A long, wide woolly article resembling a cross between a scarf and a blanket ... do as a pillow. A large cake, two packets of chocolate and fifty fags. Hum, won't go far among ten. A pot of jam—go fine on the cake or may tackle it with a spoon. And a brief note hidden away at the bottom—"For my boy."

God, how it hurt. What surging memories of a mother's love, of a mother's eternal tender care, swarmed up mistily before the eyes. Secretly, half-ashamedly, are such missives carefully put away. The mind vividly pictures the animated packing by willing hands in the humble homestead—a lump forces its way into the throat. But *war* is *war* and in it sentiment has no place.

24

CHAPTER 3

Cambrai Rehearsals—November, 1917

Uproar was rampant in one of D. Company's huts. Mingled laughter and arguments formed the base of a volume of sound materially assisted in high note effect by the banging of spoons on mess tins.

"An' now listen agin," said Tich, commanding and obtaining silence by turning over his "Press", "some more exemptions. Just listen to this 'ere summary. Six months' renewable. Six months 'ere again. An' 'ere's a poor blighter wots only got three months. Wot *are* the Tribunals doin' to give 'im so short a time before 'e goes to the cruel wars?" He paused to join in the ironical outburst that ensued and continued at the top of his lungs: "There are twenty cases 'ere an' eighteen of 'em 'as some more extensions. I ask you, boys, are they playin' fair to us at 'ome?"

"No! No! No!" in mighty chorus.

"But do we want them chaps out 'ere?"

"No!"

"They would disgrace the Bat.?"

"Yes!"

"Becos they ain't got any guts in 'em?"

"No!"

One of the two Guernsey scouts from Headquarters pushed open the door and in the general pause said:

"Heard the latest?"

"Now, no funny games," Tich ejaculated.

"Not at all. We're going up the line again."

"Oh, 'ell," said Nabo, "wot for?"

"Stunt. Another Big Push."

"Oh, 'ell," repeated Nabo; "'ere, scout, goin' back to H.Q.?"

"Yes."

"Then tell 'em I'm indisposed—ain't 'ad a long enough rest yet. An', 'ere, lets 'ave a fag. Wot with that there news and my bad 'eart for war...."

Nothing is left to chance in the offensive movements undertaken by that unparalleled fighting mechanism disposed of in two words: British Army. In following out the general scheme of perfecting every minor detail, the Cambrai attack had more than its share of elaborate preparation. Beyond the fact that a "Push" was to be inaugurated upon an entirely new and experimental form of advance, nothing was disclosed even to the men. The utter importance of maintaining absolute secrecy of this meagre information was earnestly reiterated. The slightest inkling of the impending intentions escaping to Fritz would have cast upon the troops engaged a disaster perhaps unequalled in the annals of even this Armageddon.

Following customary procedure the offensive was rehearsed mile for mile even as in the actual undertaking; aeroplanes being allotted to Divisions for scouting and observation.

The whole cycle of operations outlined by the G.H.Q. can be briefly summarised as follows: The entire movement of troops, guns, and tanks by *night* and to remain under cover from enemy 'planes during daylight. An abrupt massing on a nine-mile front of the engaging force during the night prior to launching of tanks and infantry. A furious bombardment would be opened by artillery at daybreak. Three tanks per Battalion moving forward would crush gaps in the enemy barbed wire through which advancing lines of infantry would pour into the Fritz trenches. The forward movement throughout the day to be carried on in relays of three Divisions, the final Division attaining and digging in as its objective. The Ten Hundred, forming the place of honour on the left flank of the 29th Division had to carry an objective situated, of all difficult places, on the crest of a long rise in the ground—Nine Wood.

At Brigade Headquarters a huge map was built on the ground complete to the most minute of details. From aero photographs the entire area, confined to the activities of the 86th was plainly portrayed for inspection and explanation to the Platoons. Fritz trenches, wire, observation posts, lines of support and communication; the rise and fall of the ground; villages; were all emphasised upon until Tommy became to a certain degree familiar with the ground over which Fritz had to be bundled back five miles in one day. Points where, possibly, a stubborn resistance might be offered were indicated and the advisability of *avoiding* open breaks in enemy wire constantly reiterated. (Obviously, if openings are voluntarily left here and there in the second line of wire, to one cogent factor only can such procedure be attributed, i.e., men will for preference make in a body for a clear passage and machine guns trained from the rear into these breaches would account for a hundred or so casualties before the men realised a trap.)

To merely undertake an offensive "on paper" only would be fatuous. Actual rehearsal over country as similar as possible to the original has to be carried out; villages and towns having to be "imagined" on the training area in the very position they filled on the actual territory.

Tanks were to be used on a scale calculated to put the wind up whatever enemy units held that sector. Approximately three hundred of these cumbersome but doughty caterpillars were to line up on a nine-mile frontage. They would be "first over the top"—in itself a life-saving factor that, had it been adopted earlier in the war, would have by a large percentage reduced the British casualty roll.

The manner in which they would precede the infantry from zero (the hour at which the advance is timed to begin) was practised over an old stretch of trenches and wiring; infantry partaking in the manoeuvre.

Throughout the Norman camp a stir of suppressed excitement and slightly apprehensive anticipation was apparent during the three days' training, in conjunction with the remainder of the 86th Brigade, for the big stunt. They rapidly grasped, after a hitch during the first day, what was required of them, attaining on the completion of the rehearsals a strong confidence in their powers to carry through their schedule.

They became conscious of an eagerness to try their mettle, to do something "off their own bat." At the end of each day the Ten Hundred swung in a long swaying column behind their band along the *pavé* roads homewards. Company after company sending up defiant echoes with the marching rallies peculiar to the Normans, they splashed noisily through the almost interconnected line of puddles. Upright, fine, free fellows: the very cream of Guernsey's manhood.

At night they were well content, after a late dinner, to crouch around the glowing brazier and talk, while Biffer surreptitiously was wont to fry the bacon he had commandeered. His arch enemy—N.C.O.'s—invariably endeavoured to trap him.

"Ere, you, where'd you get that bacon?"

"Bacon?" Biffer looked up with baby-like innocence. "'Ad it sent—ain't 'alf got a scent, too."

"Oh, an' that piece yesterday was sent, too, I s'pose?"

"Yes, same animal. 'E's got pink eyes."

"Wot, the pig?"

"Course—think you get bacon off a canary? Want a bit?"

"Well (mollified), only fat left, I s'pose?"

"No—only rind. 'Ere you are."

CHAPTER 4

Moving Up

Ten Hundred men stood faintly outlined in the purple pall of a starless night. Stripped to the very essentials of a battle—"Fighting Order" but carrying the valise on the shoulders and the haversack by the side. Steel helmets, gas masks and one hundred and seventy rounds of ammunition per man; no overcoats; no blankets; simply the rough, furry wolf-skin jacket for protection o' nights. Hoarse orders broke grotesquely on the damp air.

"Move to the right in fours ... right—!" By Companies the Normans moved away; glancing for the last time upon the dark bulk of old Hendecourt.

The Undertaking had begun.

They halted a few hours later in the semi-darkness of a siding where a great conglomeration of every corps stood leaning on rifles, awaiting instructions to board one of the grinding, jarring lines of trains that, shunting to and fro, emitted ghostly columns of white smoke high into the darkened heavens.

The Normans boarded their train, tumbling clumsily one into another over the dirty, evil-smelling floors of the cattle-trucks. Striking of matches and smoking were forbidden ... a babble of confusion and curses ensued while they sorted themselves out. It was impossible to wreak vengeance on the man who inadvertently placed his boot in your eye ... to turn abruptly in his direction would bring some other lad's rifle in your teeth. Sit tight and hold tight!

The Duo, with the scouts from other Battalions, attached Brigade Headquarters, succeeded in forcing their way into a genuine railway carriage—trust them! Almost immediately they were up to mischief. Having scrounged a tin of pork and beans they wanted to cook it. And cook it they did, despite orders re lights. A foot of rag was wrapped around a candle stump, placed in a tin (this paraphernalia they carried everywhere) and lit. For twenty minutes the "maconichie" boiled, and they then blew out the smouldering grease-saturated rag. The carriage was fitted with *fastened* windows and a *icor* of smouldering candle-rag with no outlet! The occupants were literally gassed. Coughing, spluttering, they almost choked.

"Phew," gasped Clarke, waving at the fumes, "it's aw-aw-awful." The other partner of the Duo could stand it no longer. Grasping his rifle he pushed it through the window. Crash! Then he laughed.

"Anybody want, want any beans?" he chuckled.

"Eat it, phew, yer bloomin' self."

"Ugh, not now after that—er—aroma." He threw the tin through the broken pane and added piously, "hope it hits someone."

Peronne! To march after detraining during the morning along its deserted streets, to gaze on the devastation of its large buildings, sent the mind wandering over the past. Peronne: this was the town from which Fritz had retreated "according to plan"; this was the goal towards which the British had gazed undismayed through the black months of slow progress, infinite hardship, and fast-flowing blood. But today the khaki tread rang firm on its roads. They who had gone before had made easy the way, and you, who were carrying it on eastwards, ever eastward. The knowledge stirred something within you and you were glad.

The Ten Hundred swung out of the "suburbs" up the long incline of Mount St. Quentin, travelled a few hundred yards along the crest and came to a halt near a line of tents. At no point in the sky was there any indication of enemy airmen, nor from the line did much rattle of distant guns disturb the quiet of the day. From the concussion of some far-off muffled explosion the earth trembled slightly; but these visitations, at lengthy intervals, caused little comment. From 12 to 4.30 p.m. sleep was compulsory. No man or N.C.O. was permitted to be seen outside his tent or hut until dusk fell, and with it the command to fall in for the long march northward to Equancourt.

Along one perpetual straight road, lined on either side with endless rows of weird, sighing trees whose tops converged in faint outline against the sky at an ever distant point; along one continual rough surface of hard, slippery cobble paving an almost tail-less column of marching troops, rumbling artillery and jingling transport crawled on through the darkness. It went hard with the Normans that night. Night and the silence, the mystery. Only the ring of many feet and the neigh of a startled horse. On, ever onward to the Unknown that awaits. Aye. Tommy, worn, rugged, rough Tommy, straining forward beneath the burden that was yours—how little others know how staunch and true beat that sturdy heart throbbing under its hard exterior. Step by step; left, right, left; rigid and mechanical, controlled by a mind that ceased to act and fell prey to wild fancies. You could hear them: the cooling whispers of a sea upon your Sarnia's shore ... dear little country! God's own Isle! Mental anguish and physical pain. And yet you came up—smiling.

Monday passed quietly at Equancourt, although one or two Fritzy shells bursting some few miles away with the unmistakeable *kru-ump* of his heavies set the brain working and conjured up memories.

B. Company, without the customary O.C. (Captain Hutchinson, one of the most popular officers among the men) of Company-Sergeant-Major "Tug" Wilson (another splendid fellow) were temporarily under the command of a Buff officer (Chapman). A., C. and D. commands were unchanged. 13 Platoon, so fictitiously unlucky(?), was probably the most "pally" combination in the Battalion; both N.C.O.'s and men were on excellent terms—especially with Sergt. T. Allez, one of the finest and most courageous men in the Ten Hundred. Lieut. F. Arnold was in command—another good fellow. This Platoon emerged with a very small percentage of casualties.

Equancourt was disliked from the moment the Ten Hundred made the disagreeable discovery that fatigues were rampant. Men began to vanish in all directions. Mahy, doing the glide from one Quarter-Master-Sergeant (the Q.M.S. is an individual who allots ten of you to a one lb. loaf, and who endeavours to convince you that your clothing issue must last for ever, and that you are far better rationed than you deserve. P.S.—We are officially informed that there are no Q.M.S.'s among the angels!)—to resume, Mahy did the gaby from one exasperated Q.M.S. right into the yawning arms of another. An enormous box was instantaneously bundled on to his shoulders, nearly bending him double.

"You'd better be careful with that little lot," the N.C.O. advised.

"Why?" with a gasp.

"Becos (drily) it's full of bombs." The hair crinkled upwards into the lad's steel helmet and he carried that box to its destination with all the lavish care and tenderness of a mother for her babe. Placing it gingerly down and unable to overcome the strong trait of inquisitiveness latent in all soldiers, he forced up the lid and peeped upon—two heavy sets of large transport wagon implements!

The march from Equancourt up to the "jumping off" point of the advance was neither so long nor arduous as on the two previous nights. As mile after mile was reeled off the incessant thunder of guns ten or twelve miles northward became more and more distinct, but on the sector of the line towards which the miles of marching columns were heading not a sound disturbed the night from hour to hour. The rumble of that distant artillery mingled with the jingle of unseen harness and the pad, pad, of countless feet. Hazy starlight faintly lit up row upon row of men, glinted dimly on brighter portions of the equipment and distinctly silhouetted each breath on the damp night air. A tense, silent march: nerves highly strung. A march to live long in memory.

Within five minutes of leaving the road for the downs there enveloped you that indefinable sense that a fighting area has been entered. Nothing could be seen, heard or felt, yet the proximity of trenches and wire was frequently "scented," like the first approaches of a sea after a long march inland.

Brigade Headquarters marched on—and with it the Duo—to where a long line of duck-boards led into a line of wide trenches. The Ten Hundred came to a halt in the immediate rear, received the order to lie down—and waited.

A night of wondrous calm and quiet. Within one mile of a watchful foe and not a sound. Once or twice a machine gun awoke wild echoes with brief spluttering bursts ... in silence more acute for the interruption hearts beat faster, hands tightened involuntarily about rifles.

Thus the young, full-blooded Normans awaited their first fray. Even as the mighty Ragnar Lodbrok and his fierce men in mail launched merciless onslaught with the breaking of day, so did Sarnia's young warriors look eastward for the Dawn.

CHAPTER 5

Cambrai Offensive—
November 20th, 1917

THE ADVANCE

It was just after six in the morning of November 20, 1917, and the dew lay thick on the soil. Men were quietly roused, rifles slung, and with fast tattooing pulse paused for orders. First wave "over" stamped feet impatiently in those interminable hours of waiting blended in what was only a few short minutes; an almost frenzy of anxiety to get through the waiting possessed them. Then the tanks, faintly outlined forms in the grey light, moved ponderously forward.

A nerve-straining silence held momentary sway.

From point to point at a few yards' interval a milliard blinding flashes of dull crimson flames leapt from out the gloom like one gigantic sunset, casting sinister glares in ceaseless succession upon the heavy mist. Roar upon roar, blending, echoing and re-echoing like unto the roll of countless mighty drums, throbbed in one great deafening crescendo. It was futile to count explosions: they all merged one into another. But words are fatuously inadequate and convey little.

"Stand by." Your pipe is in your mouth, unlit, empty. You don't want to smoke, really, but still ... the eye glances along the line of strained white faces. Someone *must* go under; still, it might not be you. Anyhow, if it is, funk will make no difference, so—one wild scramble over the top, an almost imperceptible pause and then forward. A cry, a fall here or there, and then on again. As in a dream you find yourself still carrying on unhurt ... it's not so bad.

The Undertaking had commenced.

The Ten Hundred moved forward grouped in artillery formation,

33

C., D., and B. Companies moving onward in that line from right to left; A. Company and Battalion Headquarters followed in reserve.

The staggering surprise of the British attack completely shattered the morale of what German elements were holding the sector. They surrendered in twenties to the oncoming tanks and rapidly advancing lines of infantry. Hun artillery started into frenzied action by this phenomenal development commenced to hastily lob over an erratic series of shells.

The Normans, crossing a sunken road in column, fell again into correct formation on the higher ground, progressed a few hundred yards beyond what had an hour before constituted the Fritz front line, and halted. Four light shells burst around and about the reserve Company; no one stopped anything. One piece of iron crashed into a boulder near Le Page's foot. He sprang a yard into the air and nearly put two men out of mess with his bayonet. In the hot argument that ensued they almost forgot that there was a war on and that the advance was moving on without them.

A lad with half a leg hanging and placed by two bearers on a stretcher, rose from a lying posture as the Royal Guernseys passed.

"'Ere, Guernseys," he hailed, "I was with you at Canterbury—Buffs. Jus' got in the way of a Blighty. Anybody got a fag?" It was supplied and the party moved on. About to descend into the sunken road the bearers ducked to that fatal shell whine ... too late. Three blood-soaked figures were visible through the lifting-smoke stretched inert on the ground.

"If only 'e 'adn't stopped," muttered several hoarsely. Life is chance!

The first great onslaught of artillery fire slackened towards midday, sharper crack of rifles and wicked splutter of machine guns becoming for the first time noticeable. Enemy shells became fewer and fewer, his power of resistance—weak from the opening—deteriorated to little more than a rout. The prisoners were swelling an already long roll ... nine or ten thousand on the nine-mile front.

Ribecourt, on the Normans' front, had fallen after a brief skirmish, the German last line of defence reached and artillery support was still far to the rear when the Ten Hundred, passing through the Division ahead, took upon their own shoulders the responsibility to carry the Push through its last two miles and to force the capitulation of Nine Wood, now plainly visible at the top of the next long incline.

They went for it, hell for leather, in a long line of skirmishers. Their rifles cracked with the rapidity that tells the marksmen—

and they *could* shoot. But Fritz would not have any. They did not like (those who had time to look back on their record sprint) the nasty gleam of those Norman bayonets. It was a soft thing; they moved onwards unchecked even as during the rehearsal. Tanks ahead reached the hill-crest and stood black and ugly against the sky; further to the right one was burning with high leaping flames. The Normans panted up the slope, poured into the two quarries in one bloodthirsty rush to find "nothing doing," scrambled out again, and reaching the Wood's edge calmly pushed their way through with all the phlegm of veterans to their objective some thirty yards beyond the last row of trees and commenced to dig in. Someone spotted a sniper post, coolly stretched himself out on the ground, muttered: "Three hundred yards," and squinted along the sights. Ping, ping ... two bodies fell limp from a platform—up a leafy tree. The Private slowly cut two notches on his rifle-butt.

Two black, charred figures grinned hideously from out of the smouldering remains of a British aeroplane as the two Guernsey Brigade Scouts hastened back to their Headquarters, to report the objective carried with *only ten casualties.* Away by the narrow bridge above Marcoing one living and three dead machine gunners were lying in a mangled heap. Still further back a shattered lad, unable to move, stretched out right in the track of an oncoming tank, shrieked frenziedly for succour ... then abrupt silence as of a whistle shut off even while the eyes were riveted fascinated on the inexorable crushing machine. A ghastly heap of tangled, mutilated bodies, unrecognisable as such except by the grey German uniform, were lying beneath a tank blown in by a shell—the crew huddled inside in a gruesome mass.

At the bottom of a hollow a grey-cloaked figure was bunched in that strange posture bearing the hall-mark of fast approaching death. His dull eyes filled with terror at the sound of my footsteps ... strange ingrained knowledge of the Hunnish method of dealing with similar cases pervaded his mind.

"It is—finish," he whispered pitifully in bad English.

"Where are you hit?" He shook his head slowly.

"It is finish," he reiterated weakly.

"Want anything—any water?"

"No." A battery of artillery rumbled noisily down the adjacent roadway. His eyes brightened.

"You never win," he muttered, defiance strong in his tone. But one glance took in those stoic mounted Britishers, five miles deep in the enemy lines, yet unexcited, unmoved. Thus would they fall back thirty leagues if need be, phlegmatic and unconcerned—knowing not when defeated and therefore never beaten.

"I think we will if—"; but life had passed from out the other's tired body. A rush of pity surged over one on looking into the pale boyish face: eighteen, perhaps nineteen. Little grey, bloodstained German warrior in the first flush of Youth: honour to you for the life you gave your Fatherland; for the staunch patriotism so high in your breast. May the Dawn into which you were ushered while a foe watched your passing have great compensation.

Near the unscarred Crucifix a diminutive khaki figure, an inch or so shorter than his rifle with bayonet fixed, stood peering haughtily from beneath a steel helmet, several sizes too large, balanced on his ears.

"'Allo, Guernsey," he greeted, "what price my tame outangs?" indicating a dozen grubby prisoners, "this one yere swallowed 'is false teeth wiv fright an' this porker yere 'as got 'is knees out of joint wiv shaking."

"Why are they holding up their—?"

"Oh, becos I cut the braces. Even a prisoner won't run away if his trousers are *coming down*. Nar then, Jerry—march. *No comprene?* Pushey alongay roadie *pour* tootsie—see?" He, fag-end in mouth, helmet far on the back of his head, rifle slung and hands in pocket, swaggered along behind his "outangs" on their journey to the cages.

In Marcoing we of Brigade established comfortable Quarters with the plentiful material Fritz had good naturedly (?) left behind for the purpose. His blankets when you have none of your own are a decided advantage. His jam, butter and potatoes were excellent eating, his spring beds utilised especially for two German Staff Officers—made a delightful sofa for two dirty, unshaven and grinning Tommies.

But his *bread*! Ye saints, the nightmare of that one rancid mouthful, not three times the customary ration of rum could rinse out the flavour: Martin, however, was of the opinion that another pint would do much to save his life, and on being refused sadly observed that he could not believe anyone could be so heartless....

* * * * * * * *

Drizzle, light during the afternoon, increased to a moderate downpour as the Normans were digging, not the elaborate sandbagged trenches so very familiar at home (and but little elsewhere),

36

but mere shallow excavations providing just sufficient cover for the body. An interesting operation provided with a little mild excitement in the form of enemy snipers, who, however, greatly assisted in the rapid and hurried completion of the work. (*N.B.*—This undertaking in training required half a morning!) Stumpy crawled up and down the line for a yard or two in the vague hope that someone might have made a hole too large; nothing doing, he started on one himself, grumbling audibly.

"That's it ... poor Tommy. Making a 'ole," pessimistically, "diggin' a grave for his bloomin' self."

Normans gaze westward where the vague grey earth meets the overcast sky. Five miles deep in less than twelve hours. The thrill of it—and what you have you will *hold*.

With the coming of the night came the reaction. Wild excitement and vim of victorious advance gave way for calm reflection and with it the certain knowledge of counter-attack. They realised abruptly that they were physically and mentally worn, the body clamoured madly for food and drink, the mind for rest and sleep. Rain trickled incessantly down each man's face and glistened in dusty beads upon foreheads, clothing at last gave way to complete saturation, and water, collecting in pools until over ankle deep, oozed slushily in and out of the eyelet holes.

Cold rapidly fastened its grip; dull agony pervaded the entire being until nothing more than a mechanical row of figures staring tiredly out upon No Man's Land, grasping rust-flaked rifles in numb, stiff hands. Thinking not, caring not, moving not—only that uncertain stare into the void. And over all the night, the wild shrieking of lost spirits in the trees, the sharp crack of an occasional rifle or fitful bursts from the poorly-timed enemy shrapnel.

Patrols were sent out into No Man's Land, groped blindly to and fro for two hours and returned in the very last stage of complete exhaustion to report "All Clear." Simple, is it not, to go on patrol from a line you cannot see towards another line you also cannot see ... sometimes you lost touch with the others and gazed round into the blackness with that primordial fear of the unknown inspired by the night. Lost! God, it nearly unmans you. With fast-thumping heart you hear the approach of guttural Hun voices ... *down* and *quiet*. At last calm thinking points out that yon burning house is in your own lines. Make for it and all is well. Aye. Scouts, does the pulse quicken even now?

What is the thin veneer of a mere nine hundred years semi-civilisation? Two thousand years before the Conquest the fierce warrior Northmen lived by the might of the halbert, fighters one and all from the days when the war-inspired mother croned of the battle-axe to her babe. And in the Normans was that Norse spirit dormant; but one night of such hardship as yet undreamt of had sufficed for an awakening.

In the dawn they looked out with nearly bloodshot eyes towards the German front. He would counter-attack, would he? Let him come!

He came! They poured one long volley into the long-coated line. It wavered, broke, thinned. At the junction with the Middlesex an Englishman gazed in unfeigned astonishment at the ugly, set features of his Norman companion.

"But," he said, "they might have wanted to be prisoners."

"Oh." Ozanne grunted, "don't want none," and squinting down the sights let loose another trio. "This," he added, "is the Great Undertaking."

"Yes, well?"

"I am the undertaker. For my job ... must 'ave bodies ... and I," grimly, "I'm getting 'em."

The other shuddered slightly. War is war, but these wild unkempt men of a strange tongue were something he could not quite grasp. Anyhow, they knew how to fight. That is all that matters.

Duggie Le Page went into No-Man's Land and pluckily brought in a wounded N.C.O. from one of the mounted regiments, but too late to save a life fast nearing its ebb.

A weakly sun crept up from amid thick grey clouds and shone wanly on the mud-spattered creatures lying each in his own water-logged trough. Hour followed hour without further sign of hostile movement from the enemy—nothing could be seen of him, and had the cavalry got through the attack could have been continued and Cambrai taken.

Casualties (the supreme sacrifice in two instances) began to trickle away from the Norman ranks, the majority from the attention of a sniper in the long grass who held on alone with plucky audacity. Unfortunately for his own welfare he was over-confident, exposed himself too long; and ten rifles cracked spitefully—all who fired hotly claiming the right to a notch.

Before mid-day it became apparent that Fritz had neither the heart nor the troops for launching a counter-attack on a scale large enough to make a definite impression on the newly-won area. His "strafing"

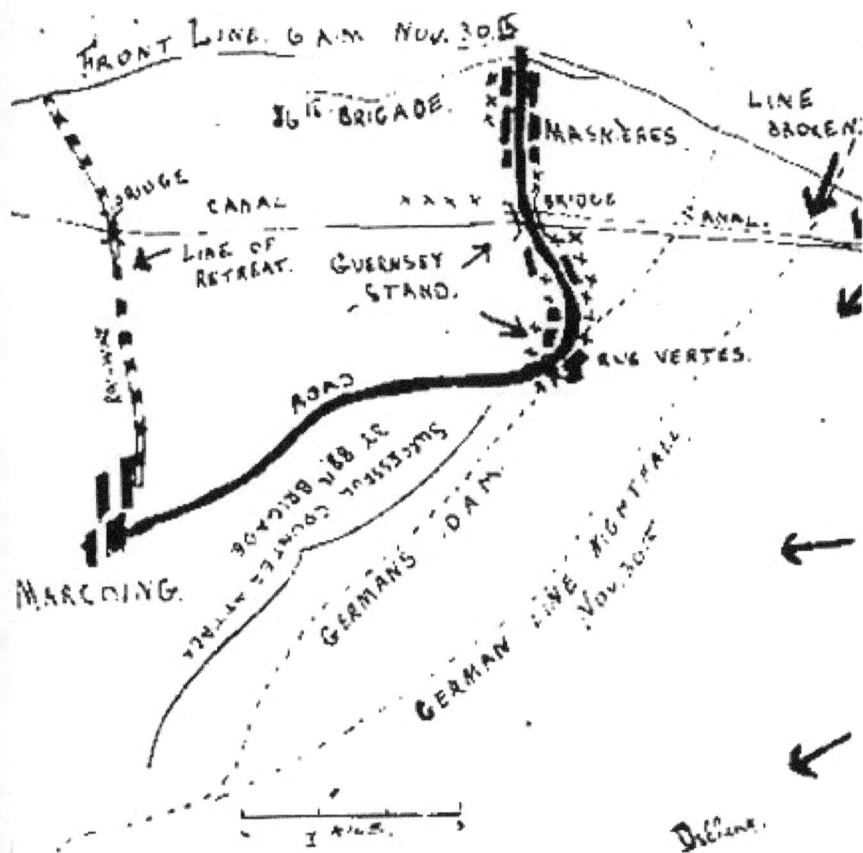

XXXX shows the approximate position of Royal Guernsey on November 30th, 1917, showing where the Battalion held with grim tenacity on to the rear, despite over 600 casualties in two days.

was fitful, poorly sighted, and of small calibre. Here and there he still had the use of a machine gun or two and had concentrated a number of men at Noyelles. This village was attacked by a company of the Royal Fusiliers; fought for desperately in one brief, mad mêlée, during which blood ran freely, but remaining in the hands of the British, formed the nearest point in the Line to Cambrai.

At Nine Wood all was quiet—except for the unearthly sounds emanating from the nostrils of one Tich sleeping in the reserve troughs with one side of his features buried in an inch of brown mud. Desultory conversation came down from the wide trough "Old man Casey" had dug and had adorned with an empty whisky bottle found in the grass. He was looking at it lovingly where it stood mouth downwards: for the obvious reason, he observed, that its spirits were like his own—all run out.

The Ten Hundred were tired, dead-beat. Marching all Sunday night, fatigue for hours on Monday, again marching in the night. Finally the attack and its holding ... eyes were heavy with ache for sleep.

Between eight and nine they were relieved, stumbled away from the wood until feet rang noisily on the rough surface of a sunken road winding Marcoing-wards.

Near a side road a number of houses were used as billet—Marcoing was untouched by shells on that date—and into these buildings Ten Hundred unshaven, unwashed, worn-out Normans entered slowly, found corners for the long-wished-for rest and threw down equipment and packs. Some jerked off boots, some faked up pillows, but the majority turned on one side, head on valise, and fell straightway into an oblivion that nothing could disturb.

Lying across a doorway, his boots and equipment still on, a veritable boy breathed regularly in the same attitude into which he had sunk the moment he had passed inside. His pale, tired face was dimly visible in the hazy starlight and one wondered at the peaceful serenity.

The last boot clattered loudly on the floor, the last rattle of a rifle placed by the owner's side, the last long-drawn sigh of relief ... Silence. Above them all Woden wove the magic spell Oblivion, the Rest of the war-worn warrior.

Daybreak had long since passed and still no sound of movement from the rows of tangled sleeping *men*. Tangle! They were lying in all directions and at every angle; it was impossible to define whose feet were whose or what had become of the chest and head of a pair of long legs leading from a jumbled heap. Duport had his feet fast in the heel of someone untraceable further than the knee—the first-named had munchers of the star-like (removable) variety. No. 2, unfortunately, struck out in his sleep, awakening the other to the fact that his teeth were promenading about at the top of his throat. He struggled to a sitting posture with a gasp, felt frenziedly for his "adjustables" and looked round upon the mixture of dirty, frowsy figures. He stirred Nobby into wakefulness by the simple expedient of tickling him beneath the chin with a grimy big toe protruding from a rent in an obsolete and far from odourless sock.

"'Ere," he said, "got any change."

"Any wha'," sleepily, "any, phew, wot a bloomin' niff. Put them blessed feet of your out of the winder. Change, wot of?"

"This yere trouser button."

"Funny, ain't it, like your face? It ole Wiffles there over the 'ead wid your rifle an' tell 'im breakfus' is up." This kindly action having succeeded, the victim looked around.

"Breakfus', where? What is it?"

"Oh, tin of Brasso; what d'you expect, 'am an' eggs or a filleted sausage."

CHAPTER 6

Marcoing—Masnieres

The Ten Hundred awoke, gazed about and laughed until the echoes rang from rafter to rafter as the eye took in each black-featured, bearded and grubby individual. Stumpy was requested to "leave that foot of fungus on his face, as it hid what for weeks had been an infliction," and to which he cuttingly replied that the other gentleman had features that would make a bomb burst.

But there could be detected in these rallies an undercurrent of strong mutual respect, of which they had all hitherto had no cognisance. They were each one intensely proud of what had been so efficiently carried out; although very little *war* was spoken they were keenly alive to the fact that personally and collectively the Ten Hundred had opened the innings with an abundance of "runs" as far as the enemy was concerned.

Rations came up fairly regularly in the advanced areas unless the ration-party becomes lost, drops a portion or makes an appointment with a 9.2. There is a constant daily issue of hard-wearing substance camouflaged as "biscuit," intended originally for the heel of concrete ships and for bomb-proof blockhouses. It can be further utilised as a body-shield, for paving roadways, or with the aid of a hammer and three chisels (why three? In case the first two break) this "biscuit" could be, and was, eaten.

Tea and sugar, enclosed in one tin, were soaked in water: boiled over a small round tin of a form of solidified paraffin, set alight beneath the mess tin.

Then bacon—Your issue might be red—and it might *not*. Perhaps the faintest suspicion of lean fringed it or you might moodily survey a square inch of fat—if there was not a buckshee inch of rind. The flowing locks of hair with which this bacon was sometimes adorned has convinced one that a number of farmers fatten their porkers on "Thatcho"—it could be combed with a fork!

Bully Beef is, ugh! IT was in the beginning, is now, and ever shall be ... *never again.*

Bread!

Something attempted, someone done,
A one-pound loaf among twenty-one.

Had the biscuit been again as hard the famished Ten Hundred would have got their teeth deep into it. Hunger. A mad craving for food that cannot be swallowed, because of a dry stickiness in the mouth a tongue that somehow would not function; a moisture that would not come.

That tea! warm, refreshing, life-inspiring liquid. Drink, to drink long and thirstily ... the relief, the new vitality. Food vanishes with abnormal rapidity, every crumb, however minute, is carefully searched for, gathered into the hand and eaten.

And afterwards you are still hungry, still thirsty.

The "schemers" slipped away quietly from the billets, crossed into the main thoroughfare and commenced a scrounging expedition for grub. ("Scrounging," an exciting operation whereby the required article is obtained by any means otherwise than legal.)

Winterflood, Mace and the Duo found their way by instinct born of experience to an advanced dressing station where buckshee tea was being doled out. Cups were not to be had, a milk can having to deputise in three instances while the fourth dug his features deep into a foot long tin with a quarter-inch layer of tea. Then Fritz dropped a shell, *kru-ump*, clean into the centre of the courtyard. The jar caused a pint of the tea to run caressingly down two tunics then again the genial enemy sent over another. *Si-izz-krump!* One of the four scroungers grunted.

"Boo—want, want any more tea?"—chuckling. They didn't! A third, a fourth, and a fifth followed. Men looked significantly at each other.

"Bringin' his guns up."

"Yes—heavy stuff, too."

"Be as hot as Hades round 'ere soon."

It was. Hun artillery were adepts at "shooting off the map" (*e.g.*, calculating the angle of elevation for concentration on a certain spot by means of a map), and began to drop near the roadways and crossroads a series of heavy calibre shells. Here and there, as his guns went searching across the town, a house crumbled under with a grinding, spluttering crash. Hun aeroplanes, also, made an unpleasant announcement of their presence above Marcoing, directing their artillery fire upon a number of points.

Our Brigade Headquarters were situated, of all unhealthy spots, in a house the last of a row culminating at a four-cross-road. Phew— and he dropped one on it and got five of us. Wilshire (Royal Fusiliers) came in for a fearful gash, ten or twelve inches long and three wide, right across the spine. Conscious, but paralysed, he looked round on us with a piteous, hopeless appeal for succour in his eyes and made wild, inarticulate sounds for water. One of the signals (R.E.) fell face downward on the floor in a widening pool of his own blood, one part of his face blown away. Poor laddies, full of youth, vim, life—cursed artillery from your far-off safety! Aye, hands clench; if ever *our* chance comes....

He played on Marcoing throughout the night, inflicted a few light casualties on the Normans, deprived a few more house of rafters, and ploughed an occasional portion of the road.

One wondered grimly on looking up at a thin slate roof what protection it would form against a "heavy," and into how many unrecognisable fragments your person would be dispersed should he land one direct on you. Close your eyes and sleep; then if he does plump one in, you won't worry much about it.

We seemed to have no 'planes of our own to interfere with Fritz's evening gambols, nor were there any Archie guns in the sector to give the Hun aviators something with which to amuse themselves.

Coloured cavalry had ridden in, out and around Marcoing throughout the day, but apparently were not going through. The advance was ended and there was every indication of establishing this new line for the quieter period of winter.

The Normans, with the 80th Brigade, moved in the evening dusk out from Marcoing to Masnières—a town that constituted almost the apex of the salient formed by the drive.

A strange march, although a mere couple of miles or so, in that throughout the entire line of companies there could be sensed some indefinable presentiment of a something to be feared. High above the direct line of march could be discerned the black puffs of enemy timed shrapnel bursting in the air. And you had to pass through it—it was inconceivable that everyone could get through unharmed. Again, it might not be you. The egotism of unconscious thought; the indisputable truth of Darwin's "Will to Life."

At Rues Vertes the Battalion halted. The nerves were highly strung, men gazed about with slight shudders as one is wont to do in the midst of weird ghost stories when someone comes softly, unexpectedly down the darkened stairs.

What was the unshakeable phenomenon? Was it the moaning of a lost wind in the dark woods that reacted so upon that rudimentary, instinctive Fear of the Unknown, the Night; inherited from the primitive man who watched trembling throughout the wakeful hours when Fear was his sole companion?

"I—I don't fancy this," Tich whispered hoarsely, "it puts a feelin' of death on me." Fatal prophecy!

The Ten Hundred carried on, crossed a swampy field, and moving up nearer the line, filed once again into the dismal occupation of trenches newly dug, affording inadequate cover and protected by wire that would have to be raised by their own efforts.

Winter was already getting a grip on the land, nights were cruelly cold and days but little better. And this first night at Masnières was frequented with that sensation of ill-omen pervading the minds of many who felt—as Tich had said—somehow that their days were drawing to a close. They would lie unmoving for an hour obsessed by their thoughts; the brain flying with its lightning rapidity from picture to picture resurrected from a happy past. In words would some communicate their apprehensions.

"I feel—rotten tonight. Something's got on my nerves...."

But the rum ration soon soared the depressed spirits. Man is prey to his inherited instincts. Even Tich recovered his nerve.

"I only felt like that once before," he said, "that's when I was spliced."

"Wot, frightened of something?"

"Yes, and," gloomily in abrupt relapse, "it came right, too." The cherubic tones of Stumpy emanated from somewhere.

"Wot I say is, respect a man's principles. Any teetotallers about yere wot wants to find a 'appy 'ome for their rum ration? Wot I say is, respe—yes, yere I am, old son, pass the sinful liquor over."

Half an hour later he warbled a jumbled melody:

"In Ari—Arizona. It's there a girl in Ari—Ari...."

CHAPTER 7

Holding the Line—Masnieres

The night was far more lively than any preceding. Fritz trench mortar batteries sending over a series of particularly nastily ranged shells. This is a type of shell that can be heard coming from far in the air and its flight, by an acute observer, can be gauged to within a dozen yards or so of the point of impact with the earth. Situated right up in the forward line this dangerous little weapon, at a range of one thousand or less (according to distance between opposing lines) yards, is fired at an almost perpendicular elevation and therefore descends again in approximately a direct line into the trenches: this factor naturally increases its probability of getting *into* the narrow excavation where a long-range shell at a more acute angle would merely dig itself into the parapet. And the havoc among human bodies confined within a small area that this small shell creates is conceivable only by those who have been of a party devastated by such a visitation. It must be borne in mind that three men can be almost obliterated by an explosion while the fourth may pick himself up dazedly, white and shaken, but unscathed. Take it as a concrete fact that any man, however courageous, who comes close enough into contact with a shell to be conscious of its hot breath on his face and to be violently thrown by its concussion, will regain his feet with shaken nerves to a degree necessitating half-hour or more before restoration to normal. Some few never recover—hence the term "shell shock."

There are tales of iron men who are unaffected by a dozen such experiences—perhaps! The writer was blown clean through an open door in Marcoing and had difficulty in keeping his hand steady afterwards to light a pipe—but he does not consider himself particularly brave. Quite the reverse. I could get round a corner with more rapidity than any man in the Battalion if a shell came my way.

46

Masnières, if external and internal appearances of buildings is a criterion of financial status, must have been peopled by a moderately wealthy class. In fairness to Fritz it must be granted that in three years' occupation he had not purloined to any large extent from the larger houses—with the exception perhaps of a few dozen clocks, a piano or two, and a few similar articles.

Though cause of this may, of course, be found in the knowledge that right up and during the British attack all these towns—Marcoing, Noyelles and Masnières—unvisited by shell fire, were still occupied by their owners. Coming up from where they had hidden trembling in their cellars during our advance, they were immediately advised to go "down the line," and in accordance trekked away from their old homes with what few personal belongings they could take with them. The road from Masnières to Marcoing was strewn with the pitiful remnants of lost bundles, which, unable to carry further, sobbing women had cast down by the wayside.

They had crowded in tearful, grateful groups around a few of the Guernsey and other battalions. Young and old. Old! Bent of shoulder, white-haired old dames; from whose kindly care-lined faces grateful tears were fast flowing, poured out volumes of thanks to the Normans in their mother tongue. Upon old backs that had long since earned repose were bundles, sad little bundles, tied up in red handkerchiefs. Ambulances were used for the conveyance of the old and spent to safety zones. Rough, big Britishers picked up the frail old frames in muscular arms, carried them with infinite gentleness to the ambulance and ensconced them securely there.

"'Ow's that, mother. A bit of all right, eh?" And the ready tears would course again down the old withered cheeks; words would not come; she could only grasp tightly on the firm young hand. How that lump *would* rise in the throat; how one fought to appear unconcerned.

Big, awkward phlegmatic Britishers; unhappy beneath all this honouring—it makes a man feel such a bally goat.

Thus the people returned to France, while on the ground near by the still figures smiled serenely at the sky. Perhaps they knew! Renouf, a plucky, good-humoured Private, walked down just afterwards with the blood dripping from his side.

The ensuing week, during which the Ten Hundred partook in wiring off the sector, completion of the poorly-dug trench system, and kindred work, was arduous not only in the physical sense, but from the constantly increasing attention of Hun airmen, artillery, and machine guns. Casualties increased, and of them Death claimed a singularly high proportion, one unfortunate Lewis-gun team coming in for a welter that shattered practically every man and ended two young lives in a fearful state of dismemberment.

Wiring constitutes in itself an operation of fatal possibilities. It has to be constructed at night, without sound; but posts have to be driven into the earth; someone will inevitably slip, accompanied by a loud clatter. Then—ping, ping, ping!!! A hundred rounds fly whining through the night from a Fritz machine-gun.

The utter wretchedness of that wiring; the sickening knowledge that any moment a trail of bullets may spring without warning at you—and if *one* machine-gun shot gets you, another *five* will be somewhere in your body before you reach the turf. It appears an impossibility to carry on alive in such an undertaking from night to night; but still you *do* it. It is funny—afterwards.

Robin hated it, after falling and introducing twenty barbs to that portion of him utilised usually in a chair; he had to reline a little to one side for a couple of days. Then blood poisoning set in, he reported "sick," and was sent down the line as a casualty.

"Of all bloomin' luck." Stumpy growled; "'ere's me wots fallen down two shell 'oles and nearly twisted me bloomin' neck, been knocked over by a shell wot capsized all my rum issue—an' not a sign of a Blighty one."

"It's a pity you didn't," Le Huray observed.

"Wot?"

"Twist yer bloomin' neck."

"Look 'ere, my lad, if I comes over there I'll twist yer tongue and tie it up behind yer 'ead, an' it wont be a Blighty yer'll 'ave—no, it'll be a blooming' corfin."

"Shut yer row, the two of you," Casey shouted, "yer like a couple wots been married a year, chewin' each others 'ead orf. Come yere an' give me a 'and, Stumpy." And he turned again to the task of clearing a layer of mud from his rifle bolt with a grimy piece of rag an inch square.

There is a refreshing originality (sic) in the *al fresco* meals partaken of in the fresh open air, in a comfortable trench—so comfortable that legs are twelve inches too long, knees in the way of your chin, and somebody's boots making doormats of your tiny bit of cheese. Water and tea—when you get it—has a most uncommon flavour of petrol due to being transported in petrol cans. Stumpy

48

was of the opinion that the War Office should be advised to utilise rum jars instead.

Fritz has a gentlemanly knack of dropping a shell near you and depositing a mighty chunk of black filth in the very midst of your grub. Resultant language unprintable.

Slight falls of snow began to take place, the wind increased and nights in the trenches became one long vista of drawn-out agony. Hands and feet froze; maintain circulation was an absolute physical impossibility: but it had to be faced through the long, over long, hours of waiting, and there was no alternative, no remedy. You suffered, Royal Guernseys, men of a warm, sunny isle, who had not hitherto known the harsh winter of miles inland spots. But you stuck it well, rifle grasped in a hand gone stiff, face cut and blistered from the fierce wind; feet aching with inconceivable agony.

Gas, sent over in shells, made an unpleasant addition to the already numerous "attractions" of the picnic. There is in this form of gas two factors that materially assist in bringing about casualties. Firstly, this type of shell cannot usually be distinguished from a "dud" and therefore alarm is rarely given until three or four of these shells have landed, by which time, if the wind is in your direction, the gas is on you. Secondly, men are careless: "Oh, the wind won't blow it this way ... might only be a 'dud,' too."

Men regard and withstand all this hardship with varying moral. There are a few who sadly collapse before the onslaught of adverse circumstances, who give way without a fight to nervous prostration, and who are subject at times to wild spasms of uncontrollable trembling, finally going down the line with a form of shell-shock altogether distinct to shock from violent concussion.

Some are stoic, hanging on doggedly; characteristic of the quiet man from tiny Sark, who, failing to understand the why and wherefore of their presence in this Hell and yet individually conscious of a sacred duty to carry on, gave a constant example of philosophic acceptance of life as it was that indicated no lack of courage. Of very similar psychological tendency were the men from Alderney—a fine, physically, body of lads, if short—and from the more remote portions of Guernsey.

The town men were adept growlers, found something funny in everything and calmly palmed off all the arduous tasks upon the good-natured but less sly countrymen. It should be recalled, however, that a large percentage of these men were "old soldiers," had seen service at

Guillemont with the Royal Irish, and were therefore au courant with every form of deep scheming.

The greater portion of the remnants of Guernsey's volunteer companies in the Royal Irish had after their first casualty been drafted into the Ten Hundred, a large proportion receiving—and rightly—promotion. They were fine types, born fighters, born soldiers, and, some of them, born schemers.

It would be futile to endeavour to convey that nowhere in the Ten Hundred were found men in whom a white streak was obviously apparent. White of face and faint of heart; the first to avoid any undertaking where their skin was endangered: crouched far below the parapet, and who at the least indication of enemy activity gazed frenziedly rearward at the nearest line for a headlong retreat. One in perhaps every hundred.

Fear, the instinct to guard life; the warning of danger; the all-absorbing sense of primitive ancestors who have handed down an almost uncontrollable Fear of the Unknown, indelibly imprinted upon the brain and imbibed into the very blood from centuries of fearful watch upon the Death that came out of the Darkness.

The fear of death overcome, there grasps the young warrior in a sudden frenzy the revelation that in some critical moment he "might funk it." There lies the crux of it. Afraid that he might *be afraid* and bring upon him from the lips of those whose opinions he values most the fatal slur "Coward." For death is far better than that those men who have placed upon you—and you upon them—the implicit reliance of *man* for *man*, should find you wanting in the test and pass sentence upon you that a lifetime regret could not one whit abate.

Two hundred, perhaps three hundred, yards from the Front Line a Fritz blockhouse (a concrete, more or less shell-proof fortress, impervious to rifle and machine gun fire, utilised on a large scale by the Germans and garrisoned with machine guns) held an advantageous position bearing on the lines of communication leading up from Masnières, thereby playing pretty havoc upon ration parties and all movement within focus of the enemy machine-gunners.

It *had* to be taken, without artillery support. The Ten Hundred were nearly let in for the job, but owing to alteration of date the Lancashire Fusiliers had the onus upon them.

Surprise was the great deciding factor.

It failed! Creeping over through the night one half of the journey was accomplished ... in one piercing whine of spiteful machine-gun fire Fritz almost wiped out the first wave. For an hour the British tried again and again with constantly refilling gaps, while upon them was turned every German machine gun in the area. From half a mile away the creeping line of advance could be gauged by the tone of firing. Higher, higher, in one mad high-pitched shriek, ten thousand shots in one minute from twenty or more enemy machine-guns sang and hummed in the inky pall. The high key lowered; the mind pictured the khaki line retreating, reforming—forward again. Then up again the shrill staccato; line drawing nearer. Higher, faster, louder the Satanic scream of lead. Higher, still higher! The head throbbed, beads glistened on the brow—surely the climax was reached. And then it lowered—failed again.

A minor operation, of no importance to Official Report!

In a field near Brigade Headquarters an unfortunate cow had investigated the explosive powers of a 9.2, with the result that it no longer had to waste its days chewing the cud. We cut away steaks by bringing the bayonet into service, but had no fat in which to fry the savoury article. The more tender portions were eaten raw—we were hungry—and the remainder fried with water and a tot of rum. A rum steak—it was "rum," inflicted us with gumboils for a week.

Some of the cheese now being issued found its way up without a ration party and upon approaching Brigade caused a false alarm of gas to be sounded. It has been found effective in poisoning lice. This little adherent is now in dozens upon every other fellow. Folk at home have a peculiar tendency for sending out powders, for the entertainment of these pests, upon which they wax fat: dying sometimes of constipation.

The mail had arrived on the Thursday night (November 28th) that the Ten Hundred came out of the line for the last time. The Division will move, out on the morrow after nearly two weeks' marching and fighting. Casualties had increased: the Lanes, and Royal Fusiliers numbering but little over 500 men. (They entered the action about 700 strong.)

The Normans had lost between forty and fifty, inclusive of several Supreme Sacrifices. Muray had one eye blown out by shrapnel from a trench mortar without losing consciousness.

A draft should have joined the Battalion, but halted for the night in Rue Vertes, coming in for a bout of shelling that put the wind up the entire party, with inflicting much bodily harm.

A strange non-appearance of British 'planes has caused comment, nor did there appear to be any heavy guns remaining on the sector apart from such artillery that forms a Brigade complement. Fritz, on the other hand, maintained uncomfortable concentration upon the towns and roads with a large number of guns brought up from somewhere (Lille—where an Army Corps had been awaiting transfer to Italy). The number of gas shells indicates that his supply in this direction is unlimited, for this type comes over regularly day and night. He concentrated, too, upon the canal lock in the probable vague hope of flooding the district. His shells fell by the scores around, above, short of and beyond the objective, everywhere except, by extraordinary bad luck, upon it.

CHAPTER 8

November 30th-December 1st, 1917 —German Onslaught

4.30 a.m., Friday, November 30th.—Quiet, comparative quiet everywhere. Gas shells came over with an ever increasing frequency, but men slept on without masks. A shell, heavy, unmistakably from a huge howitzer, crashed with a mighty uproar into a small house and demolished it at a stroke. Then another, and another, and still another ... phew, what was he "searching" for? From the doorway of Brigade Headquarters I looked into the night and listened to the whistle of shells passing overhead from eastward into our lines. Our own artillery was silent. No sound came from our near infantry lines, not the crack of a rifle, not the splutter of a machine-gun.

Again the dull drone of the heavy stuff—the practised ear could gauge its fall, and I retreated a few yards into the passage. The courtyard outside caught it, and the entire chateau trembled violently at the concussion. But why, why these big guns? Another landed in the yard, followed by an unearthly tinkle of falling glass. Someone ran in from the gateway with a headlong rush, gained the passage and paused.

"Phew," excitedly, "what the devil is Fritz up to? Heaviest shells on this front."

"Yes. Might be coming over."

"Hardly."

"Why these heavies?"

"Dunno. He's shelling along the whole line—good God," in a shout, "look at that chap there ... it, oh, my God, it's got him ... did you, did you, see *that?*" A heavy had whined into the yard just as a runner essayed a blind rush. Nothing was left. Nausea, a slight dizziness enveloped us.

"What," he asked hoarsely, "what is this place?"

"86th Brigade."

"I want the Guernseys."

"In the Catacombs. The road up on the right." He walked out on to the steps, stared intently into the night—in a flash we both sensed Death. He ran down the flight:

"Good-night." He was a death casualty that night, and we *had both known it.*

Presentiment of looming danger was pregnant, became accentuated with the increase of heavy shelling falling from three angles: from directly overhead, from the right rear flank and left rear.

It all culminated before dawn into a barrage on our lines, shells raining in on every acre by the dozens. From the top of the chateau (it was built on a hill) with the coming of day, wave upon wave of grey-coated infantry could be discerned through the glasses. It was impossible to estimate their number, line followed line in such rapid sequence that the eye was bewildered.

They were up against the 29th. The Division wiped out, not partially but completely, row after row. Rifles and machine-guns mingled in hasty chorus, incessant, rapid, accurate. Fritz fell back.

The glasses swept over to the right: the heart gave one wild leap of anxiety. The Division on the right had to face an advance it was unable to stem, a first line had fallen and a bunch of khaki figures were being hurried away into the German rear. Beneath pressure too heavy the line gave, retired rapidly, and the 29th's flank was exposed at a mere *half-mile's* distance.

A call was given for a Guernsey scout ... from the passage an inferno of shells were visible bursting every few yards, instantaneously the mind formed: "Impossible to go through alive." One wild frenzied run across the vibrating yard, hearing everywhere the thunderous bursts, fumes fouling the nostrils, breath coming and going in gasps; running like Hades, bent almost double: any second the singing pieces of shrapnel flying past will get you. Into the Brigade Headquarters with a wild laugh! You're through, but you have got to get *back*.

In response to that message the Ten Hundred turned out.

They swung out into Masnières' cobbled hill, rifles slung, and marched with all the nonchalance in the world towards the bridge, cigarettes and pipes going, laughing and joking—thus have I a hundred times watched them go on parade.

That march, a classic; let it go down into history as an emblem of the old Ten Hundred. Their last march together, their last foot chorus on the long trails. Square of shoulder, upright, I see even now those figures that have long since been still. Every yard a man crumpled up, any yard it might be *you*. And they laughed and smoked, went forth to call "Halt!" to those waves of grey, advancing some hundred yards away, as if they had a hundred lives to give. Let coming generations marvel. The Farewell March of the First Ten Hundred. Before the sun had reached its noon many had crossed the Great Divide and passed the portals of Valhalla to swell the throng of their Viking forefathers.

The enemy advance had continued with remarkable rapidity towards Rues Vertes and Marcoing. Rear Brigade Headquarters, in Rues Vertes, or at least above that village, had been seized, and the R.E.'s, a portion of the N.C.O. staff, all rations and ammunition captured. A dressing station filled with R.A.M.C. and wounded was taken, but Frit acted honourably, placed a sentry over the entrance and allowed the Red Cross men to carry on with their work.

From Marcoing the 88th Brigade formed a line running towards Masnières, and with the dull, wicked bayonet went out to meet the grey forces. Here and there bayonet met bayonet. Again it was the 29th. Blood poured into pools on the grass, Hun after Hun clasped his weakening grip upon the British bayonet rasping through his chest. He fell and with a foot on the body for leverage a red, dipping blade was withdrawn. On again, crack! crack!! Lunge, until the ribs snapped like dry sticks beneath each thrust. Stoic British, unmoved, unexcited ... well might you Germans call the 29th the Iron Division. Aye, the Cult of the Bayonet!

The enemy sickened ... ran.

Lining the roads above and below the broken Masnières bridges, with its half sunk tank, the Ten Hundred pumped an annihilating shower or lead into the lines of enemy creeping along the canal bank. He turned and retreated, but a swarm of grey figures had taken Rues Vertes and were consolidating their positions in what constituted a direct menace to both the 88th Brigade at Marcoing and the other two (89th and 87th) holding on against the onslaught on a line stretching from Masnières to Nine Wood. In this village the enemy held a pivot from which a turning movement, if supported with sufficient troops and guns, could be enforced. He had both these essentials and his aeroplanes grasped in a moment that an advance from here would, if successful, bring the Hun infantry into the direct REAR of those British lines still intact, cut the only line of retreat and force the capitulation of the Divisions at the apex of the salient.

Fritz 'planes were up in scores flying in formation, and, having no opposition, were frequently at an altitude of a mere sixty or eighty feet. The scouts, peering down on the situation at Masnières, took in at a glance the wide area that had to be covered by the solitary Norman Battalion without support of any kind. This information was communicated to the German Command. Inroad from Rues Vertes was prepared with certain confidence; but they had not calculated with the Normans and before the Command could move a finger *they had lost Rues Vertes!*

There was not in that first storming of the village the desperate hand-to-hand fighting that would inevitably have ensued had the Hun made a stand. The Normans scampered wildly into the one narrow road in the stop-at-nothing rush that came naturally to them; some slipped down the fields with Lewis-guns, and Fritz aware that his left flank was falling back before the grim counter-attack of the 88th, retired with abrupt haste. The Lewis-guns (a machine gun firing 700, or slightly over, shots a minute—in theory, 500 in actual practice) in the fields found that the German retreating line was by force of circumstance brought into that most-deadly fire, enfilade (e.g., firing across a line from a point of vantage at the flank). The guns opened without warning on the three waves, more or less in mass due to the involuntary retreat. No more adequate simile can convey the picture of the fast-falling figures than that of grass beneath the scythe. Five minutes, perhaps ten, and it was over. Bodies lay thick everywhere, and upon this area of wounded and dying shells were casting square feet of flesh yards into the air.

German 'planes, viewing this massacre from above, swept down in swift retribution, and flying low turned their machine-guns upon the unprotected Normans. An aeroplane travels at anything from eighty to one hundred miles an hour, and this very speed restricted a lengthy concentration on any one spot, but many a Norman fell forward on his face, a dozen leaden bullets in his skull and chest.

Duquemin, conscious and moaning piteously in agony, was lying crosswise over his rifle, one leg smeared with blood, and the other reclining grotesquely against the hedge twenty yards away. Doubled up on a hedge top, rifle still levelled at the foe, a figure lay and upon its shoulders a ghastly mess of brains and blood crushed flat in the steel helmet. Duval stumbled blindly towards the dressing station, the flesh gleaming red down one side of his face and an eye almost protruding. Le Lièvre limped away in the direction of Marcoing and walked for five hours before succour came his way. Tich was lying face earthwards near the Crucifix, a rifle shot in the very centre of his head. Rob, quiet, gentle-natured Rob, fell forward against the semi-trench.

"I—I've got in—the head," he said weakly "I—I'm going, go—." He collapsed ... life ebbed away and he was still.

But the Normans held Rues Vertes.

The Germans launched a heavy offensive, for the retaking, wave after wave, line after line, moving ponderously forward. The Norman rifles and machine-guns shrieked out lead in a high staccato until the advance, slackened, wavered and fell back. Hun artillery showered shell, gas, and shrapnel over every yard of ground. For a period the Normans fell in dozens everywhere. The canal in places was stained red, and Norman bodies drifted twirling away on its fast-running waters before sinking.

Ammunition was short. Scouts from Headquarters tried to get into Marcoing with the information. Clarke moving along the road found himself unable to return or to move because of a Fritz advanced post. One of the Middlesex crossing a clearing in the trees was wiped out by machine-gun fire and toppled over into the canal.

Mighty trees, a yard radius, bordered those waters, but at every few paces forward the eye took in one of these monsters split open by a shell. The pulse quickened; if it did that to a tree what would be left of you—anyhow you wouldn't know much about it. Approaching Marcoing the hum of an aeroplane, flying low sounded—in a second I feigned casualty, but he got home on the other scout ahead. Phew, wind up!

The very streets of Marcoing were almost obliterated by the jumbled heap of stone, wood-work and bricks lying across them. Bodies in every inconceivable state of partial or whole dismemberment made a ghastly array in the bleak sunlight, blood from man and animal formed dark pools in the hollow sections of the shattered roadway. Progress could only be made by moving apprehensively close up to what walls were still standing, and to sprint wildly over the open. Wounded were streaming in hundreds towards the dressing station in the square ... many failed to reach there alive.

From the top of the Chateau in Masnières, Corporal Cochrane (the finest little N.C.O. in the Battalion) and a few others were sniping at Hun *artillery* some four hundred yards distant. *At last* had the infantryman his chance.

A steady glance down the sights. *Crack!* Miss! *Crack!* Got him but only slightly. *Crack, crack!* The unholy glee of it. You could see by the way he fell that it had gone home fatally. Crack—another five rounds are rammed into the magazine ... pump it into them, play hell with that Artillery while the chance lasts.

They stare wildly about in a frenzy. *Crack, crack, crack!* They have had enough and retreat a few hundred yards further south. Still, there lies a dozen or more who will not again pour into the quivering flesh shrapnel's hell-hot agony.

A glance along the Norman ranks during the late afternoon showed appreciably by the many gaps separating man from man how many casualties had already obtained. Shells claimed a large toll of victims even among the more or less screened rows of figures lying along the eastern edge of the canal. Le Poidevin and Le Page, lighting cigarettes from the same match, caught one in the right and the other the left leg, two flying pieces of shrapnel from a shell bursting over one hundred yards distant; fell and stared at each other in painful astonishment ... hobbled laboriously on the long journey (for a wounded man) into Marcoing.

Stumpy, secure behind a small mound, had gazed with black pessimism on life from the moment Tich had given *all*.

"Gawd," he observed generally, "ain't it orful. What with shells, an' dead, an' gas! An' I ain't 'ad any rum since last night. Wot a pore Tommy has got ter put up with."

Night. A night when men crouched over their rifle waiting to kill, when the owl had gone far from the slaughter and even not the fitful flutter of a bat sped through the dark pall. Only man: savage, primitive man, glared at where each remained hidden. The blood lust to kill, always to kill. Animal ferocity and passion: man's inheritance.

From No Man's Land came the sobbing call of wounded for succour. Far, far across the void sounded those despairing frenzied shrieks. Hoarse, appealing, incessant, until they weakened and nothing reached the ear but the smothered sobs of men whose life's sands were running out for want of that aid, so near, but which they were unable to reach.

Verey lights from Fritz's lines rose and fell with monotonous certainty, throwing faint glows on the huddled heaps lying in all directions between the two fronts. A gleam would catch reflection in the glassy eyes of a stiff form, fade and leave you staring hypnotised into the night. Was it distorted fancy ... then you would see it again, and again, until in its very frequency you noticed—nothing.

Shelling slackened. Now and again a pause when the stillness could be "heard." From the woods in intermittent intervals the one solitary gun still intact in an entire battery belched forth a lone shell into the enemy lines. In the fantastic flash of each explosion three shirt-sleeved forms showed a ruddy silhouette of blackened hands and features. A tearing, splintering crash awoke echoes as some great bough was shattered in impact with a "heavy" and crackled its cumbersome way past smaller branches to where it splashed into the canal.

Into an advanced dressing station about Rues Vertes one of the Duo stumbled, bleeding profusely from several wounds, dripping with slimy mud and water, features covered with the grey black dust that comes from close contact with a shell. Ozanne stared at him.

"Gawd," he said, "'ow'd you get that?"

"Scrap—with a Fritz outpost—got a stretcher?" He bent down in a half-faint, was carried to a stretcher and his wounds in body and arm bound. Fag in mouth he dozed, was startled into wakefulness by a call from the Padre.

"Boys," he was saying, "this village will be evacuated shortly—can't possibly hold on. Those wounded who can had better walk to Marcoing."

To Marcoing! Two and a half miles. The Norman moved dizzily out of his stretcher, stood up, and tottered to the entrance.

"Here, kid," a Corporal (R.A.M.C.) advised, "You can't do it."

"I can."

"You'll peg out on the way."

"Sooner that than—be—a prisoner. But I can—do it." He did!

Dawn! And with it an intensity of shelling over the whole area. Earth, limbs, trees were constantly somewhere in the air. Bodies of yesterday were torn asunder again and the wounded who had lasted out the night shrank and writhed in the fiery hail of shrapnel. Fritz came over again. He is a courageous warrior, not afraid of his own skin, but is at best when fighting in numbers. A lone fight, back to the wall, is not his métier; he, if at all threatened, retreats.

Rues Vertes fell.

It was a physical impossibility for the Ten Hundred to hold on. The casualties already exceeded three hundred, every man was utterly worn, hungry, had existed for twenty-four hours in a state of the highest nerve tension. Not one was there who had not missed death a dozen times by the merest of escapes. They had for ten or eleven days been engaged in an offensive and what meagre rest had been theirs was woefully insufficient to counteract the heavy demands made upon the stamina.

Out-numbered by twenty to one, completely out-gunned. No reserves, no supports, and only one small line of retreat. No aerial observation, no adequate cover, and an enemy who was aware that a mere shattered Battalion stood between them and the capitulation of one or more Divisions. They were half famished, tired out ... his troops were fresh. He had no doubts as to the result.

Again the 29th Division repelled an attack on its original front line. Fritz tried the flank, came on in waves stretching far over the hill crest. A fire stopped him—*could* there be only *one* corps before him. He rallied, swept on again, swarming over the canal banks and close up into the outer Masnières' defences; but on his lines hailed a rapid fire from the Normans, the like of which he had never deemed possible. Savident ran alone into the centre of a roadway with his Lewis-gun and poured every solitary shot by him in one long sweep up and down the wavering lines. Rifles cracked with the rapid reloading action of marksmen until the barrels burned hot in the hand. The Germans fell back. The Normans went forward in that reckless rush.

Rues Vertes was retaken!

In the outskirts of this village a number of the draft were isolated, became tangled in one great bloody mêlée with the angrily retreating enemy. There was nothing for it but a fight to the death.

Through the glasses they could be seen to hold off the Hun for a few brief minutes, met him in a ghastly lunging of bayonets, from which beads of blood were dropping ... but they went under one by one, until one thick-set lad remained, seized two Huns one after the other by the neck, twisted them with his own hands and went over the Divide, a bayonet through his heart.

But their example put the fear of death into the enemy and for an hour the thinning line of Normans had no attack.

He reformed, sent a large number of machine-guns with his first wave, concentrated a fearful artillery fire on the villages, and swept forward. The same fire met him, again the lines wavered, but that hail of lead was more than the men could withstand. They went back—many of the gunners without their machine-guns, not back a hundred yards or so but almost out of *rifle range*.

The artillery fire had created havoc among the Normans. Twenty figures writhed in agony in so many feet, a stream of blood-soaked lads were moving slowly away towards Marcoing. One Lewis-gun

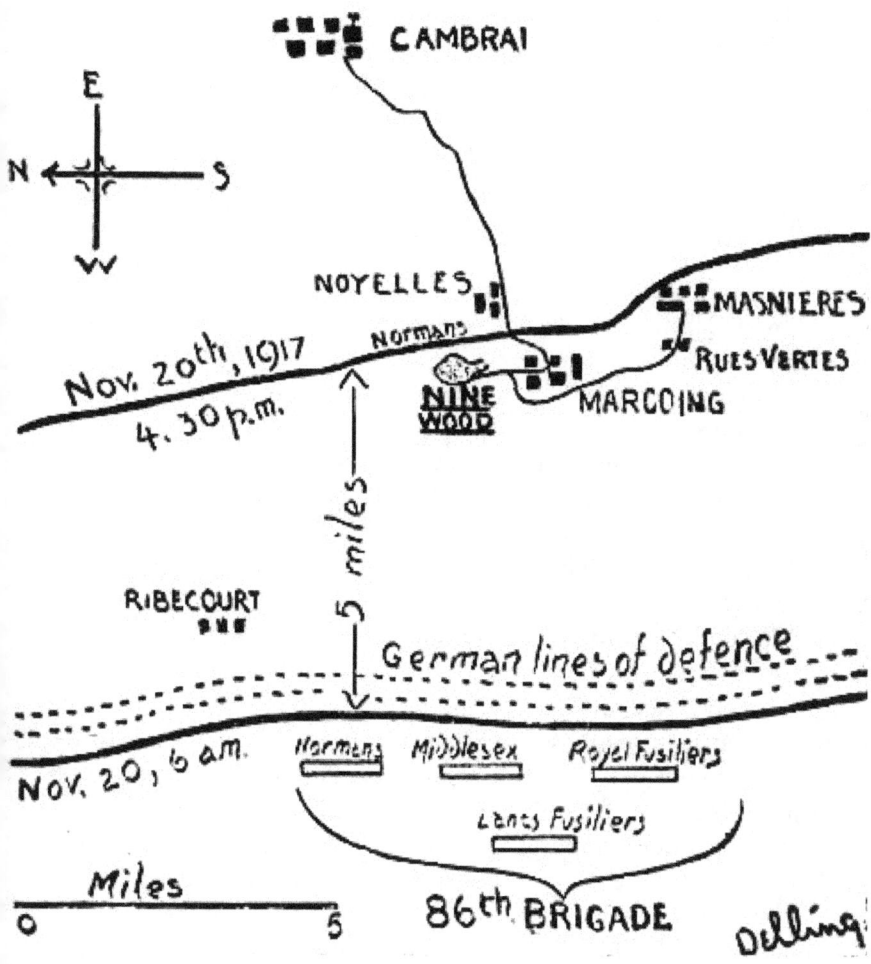

E

N — S

W

CAMBRAI

NOYELLES

Normans

NINE WOOD

MASNIERES

RUES VERTES

MARCOING

Nov. 20th, 1917
4. 30 p.m.

5 miles

RIBECOURT

German lines of defence

Nov. 20, 6 a.m.

Normans   Middlesex   Royal Fusiliers

Lancs Fusiliers

86th BRIGADE

Delling

Miles
0   5

Cambrai

team was lying about in all directions, forms distorted, limbs missing and great bare stretches of red flesh showing with sickening brilliancy of colour—and the gun itself was *untouched*. Irony of fate.

On the sloping grass seven inert khaki forms could be counted, on the lower levels another five: stretched across the mound to the east of the canal a dozen or more were visible at intervals of eight or so yards. All from *one* spot without moving the head.

The casualties were more than the untouched.

Weary Normans, knowing that *your* turn would not be long a-coming—and you would not be sorry when it did—knowing, too, that behind was no relief force. You had to *hold*, there was no alternative. And each face lifted earnestly in the light was set of jaw. God grant them life and they would hold until the Hun himself called "Halt!"

Ammunition had come up ... therefore was there only one factor by which they might fail—no men to use the rifles. They spoke sometimes in the pauses.

"Wonder wot they'll say at 'ome about all these yere dead?"

"Dunno."

"Anyhow, we ain't done bad work."

"No; an' we'll hang on yere like 'ell, even if they brings the ole bloomin' German army."

"Sure. If Jerry thinks 'e can show us 'ow to shoot 'e has made a 'ell of a outer."

"D'you know," shyly, "we 'ave done somethin' big!"

"Yes; I s'pose we 'ave."

The very men who had fought on and made good in face of odds that no man in his senses would have bet on at a thousand to one chance, opined that they had "done something big," or at least they "s'posed so."

No Regiment in the Empire, or out of it, could have done more. They had to "hang on" at any cost. They did: simply, doggedly.

The Guards—rushed up to the southern portion of the sector and launched against the German advance—with a determination and tenacity of purpose against which the offered opposition was futile, turned the enemy flank and forced them back in the direction of their original (November 30th) line through Cambrai.

A strong detachment fell back on the Masnières-Rumilly sector, thereby enforcing on the small Norman remnant a further infliction of bloody fighting and casualties. The Guards swept back the waves of grey upon the Guernseys, who could not retreat—for a few hundred yards behind them the rest of the Brigade were holding up a further enemy element.

Our own artillery, harassing the Fritz retreat, sent over a number of shells into Masnières. Fritz batteries, in response to the urgency of the situation, hailed down shrapnel on a scale only equalled on the morning of their onslaught. The Normans came in for the thick of it.

The men holding the far end of the little town found themselves swamped down in the overwhelming rush of an entire retreating Battalion. They were prisoners before the abrupt alteration in the direction of the German movement had dawned on them.

Above Rues Vertes the spiteful fire of the remaining scattered units of the Ten Hundred impressed upon the Hun mind a fear of those riflers that was pregnant enough to force him to rapidly verge away from the spot to a safer distance of a mile or so.

The little village near the Crucifix was withdrawn from at dusk with no molestation. Shelling slackened to a mere initial salvo from Rumilly. The lull followed in which enemy reinforcement were being brought up to be thrown in large forces upon those stubborn British regiments who were clinging tenaciously, with unshaken obstinacy, to shattered trenches.

Lieut. Stone (afterwards M.C.) led a bombing raid under cover of night into Rues Vertes, originating there an uproar that startled every Fritz within a mile into a bad degree of "windy" apprehension. He fired into the air a frenzied array of Verey lights in hope of discovering the extent of the raid. Had the Ten Hundred been less war-worn they would have chuckled delightedly over this successful bluff, but they hardly commented upon it, stared wearily and disinterestedly at the flashes of bursting grenades, turned away and banged arms and hands noisily on thighs to enforce some little circulation into those cold, clammy limbs.

So utterly exhausted were a few of the youngsters that they had fallen into unsettled sleep across their rifles, startled now and again into fearful wakedness by a mind that had for days been awaiting something that would inevitably come.

Men were little more than mechanical figures, but the brain ran rampant and uncontrolled until the wild memories of furious German attacks earlier in the day surged up with acute pregnancy and the victim fell prey to poignant hallucination. The endless rows of grey figures would advance yard by yard ... five hundred range, four hundred, three hundred. God, we can't stop him. The crackle of rifles and machine-guns shrieked higher ... two hundred; one hundred. Breath comes and goes in sobs—in one minute he will be on you. Then he wavers. Now is the time; pump the lead into him ... he turns.

And the lad regaining control of his distorted imagination discovers that his rifle barrel is hot and that he has let fly a dozen rounds into the void ... a shaky hand passes slowly over a sweat-covered brow.

The Higher Command, realising that the holding of Masnières with the small remnants of troops in the sector was impossible, ordered the withdrawal to a support line of the old Hindenburg system, and thus straightening out or at least modifying the British frontage.

What remaining elements of the Ten Hundred still survived were allotted the last task of covering the Brigade's withdrawal. They stood their ground to the final stages of the movement and they only evacuated because *ordered to do so*.

Middlesex, Lancs. Fusiliers, Royal Fusiliers, each Battalion badly cut up, moved away while the Normans held on, pumping lead in whining chorus to convey to the German mind that troops were plentiful and to camouflage the fact that a withdrawal was taking place.

Then they stumbled to their feet, weak from exhaustion, exposure and hunger.

The wind moaned in trees in company with their uncertain footsteps, the still forms of brother Normans smiled up to the stars and bade them mute farewell as they came away from that sacred ground, sodden with their blood. The Germans in the morning would find everywhere the honoured dead and would place them in their last resting place in the damp soil for which they had willingly given of their *lives* to hold.

Because no one would be there to resist him he would walk their treasured strip of soil; but his footsteps would never have defiled it while *one Norman* had remained.

Hands clenched in agony ... he would take it ... they had failed to uphold those who had gone before. To leave it after all they had done, to give it without a shot. Why, why—?

The Passing of the Old Ten Hundred.

A few over three hundred men marched without sound to where a train awaited. Silent, haggard, worn!

The remnants of the Normans. Six or seven hundred casualties in two days—they were aptly "remnants."

The train pulled out. The Cambrai Offensive was merely history.

The following letter was sent to the Bailiff of Guernsey by the C.O. of the 29th Division shortly after the Cambrai battle, which the Bailiff read at a sitting of the Royal Court:

I want to convey to the Guernsey authorities my very high appreciation of the valuable services rendered by the Royal Guernsey Light Infantry in the Battle of Cambrai. Their's was a wonderful performance.

Their first action was on November 20th. and though their task of that day was not severe, they carried out all they were asked to do with a completeness that pleased me much. The C.O., De La Condamine, was then invalided, and I placed my most experienced C.O. in command. This was Lieut.-Colonel Hart-Synot, nephew of Sir Reginald Hart.

On November 30th, when the Germans, in their heavy surprise attack, pierced our line to the south of my sector, the enemy entered the village of Les Rues Vertes, a suburb of Masnières, which town was my right flank. It was the Guernsey Light Infantry which recovered this village twice by counterattacks, and which maintained the southern defences of Masnières for two days against seven German attacks with superior forces and very superior artillery. When we were ordered to evacuate Masnières on the night of December 1st, it being a dangerous salient, with the enemy on three sides, it was the Royal Guernsey Light Infantry which covered the withdrawal. Guernsey has every reason to feel the greatest pride in her sons, and I am proud to have them under me fighting alongside my staunch veterans of three years' fighting experience.

Many officers and men greatly distinguished themselves, among whom I may first mention Le Bas, and after him Stranger, Stone and Sangster.

I enclose a copy of Special Order, and feel that Guernsey should participate in the pride we all feel in having done our duty. I regret the casualties of the Battalion were heavy, a further proof, if any were needed, that they fought magnificently.

CHAPTER 9

December-January, 1918—Houvin

Detraining at a railroad the small force of Normans swung away upon a long march to billets in Houvin, partaking at last of the rest that had for so long been their dire need.

The plenitude of food, ample sleep, clean clothing, and the wholesome cleanliness of pure water in which the body could be purified of a war's protracted stagnations, acted visibly upon the spirits. They had had access to papers portraying to the full how much had depended upon their stand in those critical days, and now it was over they marvelled at how they had done it.

From their connection with the 29th Division, in the previous September, there had been borne upon them from friendly contact with brother Battalions, the subtle esprit de corps permeating a Division who had won fame at Gallipoli, who inspired when transferred to France a fear of their arms in the Hun mind, and won from the recalcitrant foe eulogy in the form of "The Iron Division."

A strong mutual respect was apparent between them and the remaining regiments of the 86th Brigade. Each felt that reliance could at any time be placed upon the other: had they not already put their mettle to the test and come through with honours?

The old humour re-asserted itself among the wild, careless fellows who had come through. Tich, one of the Duo, Birfer, and Ginger were no longer there to plot out their daily round of "schemes." Clarke, Martel, Stumpy, and Old Casey were left to carry on—and they were quite capable of doing so.

Stumpy formed a friendship with another of his diminutive height and large waistband in the Middlesex, and the two were frequently hobnobbing together in each others' billets.

"We lost a lot of good fellows," Stumpy sighed heavily over his pipe, "wot we couldn't spare. There was three wot never drank rum and who all got 'it." A roar of laughter interrupted him. "Yes, all got 'it. And there was pore old Jack who got a dose in the arm an' 'ad to walk a 'ell of a way to the dressin' station. 'E was bleedin' bad an' asked me ter take orf 'is pack, which I did, an' his water-bottle as well, becos it was full of rum and—an' rum is 'eavy."

"Rum, full of rum," his little pal looked up at him with dry lip, "you—you ain't got any left?"

"No, becos I put it aside, an' some scrounger pinched it. All I 'opes is that it bloomin' well choked 'im." Someone bawled from the doorway that "supper was up."

Billets are a form of barracking troops in a number of barns and stables spread over as small an area as possible. The one salient advantage of these shelters is fresh air; it comes in with icy gusts through these apertures made for the purpose and whistles through cracks in the door—if there is a door—and gaps where once glass had kept it out. For those to whom the sky on a star-lit night provides an hour's ecstasy a hole or two in the roof is a blessing, but to the common mortal is a damnation by which the winter wind tints the nose o' nights a soft shade of deep purple or gives passage to a gentle flow of rain that forms lakes and pools on your overcoat and blanket and which at the slightest movement runs like a small river down your chest until you wake with a shivering gasp.

Rats and mice make their way interestedly in and out of sleeping forms, investigate with deliberate intent the contents of your pack, or perchance make a tentative nibble at an odd toe or so. If anything digestible is found in an overcoat pocket the exasperating rodents do not enter by the obvious pocket-flap, but *chew* their way in from the outside.

The weary old monotony of daily routine common to the Army set in, parades and inspections forced their unpleasant encroachments upon each day. Men whom a few weeks before had been forced to face the heaviest fighting they had ever experienced, now made the abrupt discovery that they were again liable to fall foul of the miles of red-tapeism that is everywhere rampant in Regulations respecting innumerable minor offences.

This perpetual inspection by an officer sickens. His minute survey of every inch of the uncouth, Army-rigged mortals, peppered with injunctions in relation to an absence of polish on boots or equipment, was never favourably received. There was a grain of humour in the actions of subalterns who were wont to jab up and down the bolt of a rifle with the air of an expert and solemnly inform the owner (who had fired several hundred rounds through it at tight moments) that he must "... be careful to oil the bolt—most important."

Much new clothing had to be issued to replace the battle-scared remnants of the Cambrai stunt. Thrown to the men in the happy haphazard Army method—there were created a new series of Parisian modes for draping the figure. Army-rig! There was no lack of space or originality in the cut of Le Huray's enormous wide trousers (the leg would comfortably have encircled his waist), turned up when worn without puttees two and one-half inches at the bottom; the top if hitched well up had manifest advantages as a muffler. Issued on the same logical lines, Mahy received a tiny pair of nether garments for his loner legs and a little tunic that hung limply like an undersized Eton-jacket six inches short of where it should have reached. Some lads were lost in shirts with sleeves generally associated with Chinese or other Eastern gentlemen, others moodily surveyed themselves in small shrunken garments that with only superhuman effort could be forced to meet the waistband without emitting a warning rip. Duport found it so.

"Look 'ere," he growled, "trousers won't reach me waist upwards; shirt won't either, downwards. Leavin' a bloomin' two inches orl round of bare flesh."

"Camouflage it."

"'Ow d'you mean?"

"Paint the space brown an' pretend it's a belt."

The Quarter-Master Sergeant and his assistant found an avalanche of new material and old on their hands. (The Q.M.S.'s are those individuals who keep *all* the new clothing in store and by only the wiliest of Tommies can such material be wangled.) The Q.M.S. of the Ten Hundred was not exactly popular among the ranks. N.B.—Neither Q.M.S.'s nor C.Q.M.S.'s are acquainted as a rule with the gentle solitude of the first line trenches. Their duty it is to receive and issue the "plum and apple," the "road-paving" biscuit and the weekly change of under-garments.

In the Field no man has actual possession of shirt, sock, or under-garments. These are all given in at each visitation to the baths and others issued in return. Your shirt thrown over to you by the C.Q.M.S. might be somewhat decrepit and holey or might have some resemblance to a new one. You might have two odd socks or (if you were among the bevy of schemers) two or three pairs would be in your possession—illegally.

Parades were detestable. They had imagined that England was the training camp for these operations. In France they had expectation of fighting and resting, *not* marching up and down with occasional halts, while the Platoon Officer furtively asks his sergeant what order he must give next.

The pivot round which all parades manoeuvre is always with the Regimental Sergeant-Major (the main function of all R.S.M.'s is to walk round with a big stick). He, an old Regular, despite the iron discipline so candidly hated, was withal a staunch supporter of fair play for the ranker, a tartar on parade, and feared more by the junior N.C.O.'s than the very inhabitor of lower regions.

An N.C.O. (Non-Commissioned Officer) is an individual whose main talent lies in the ability to bawl out orders at men one yard distant in a voice having a hundred yards range. The possessors of some subtle superiority not discernible by ordinary individuals, they are for this reason forbidden to converse or walk with the men when "off parade." These stringent regulations never materialise in actual practice, but it conveys a hint of the tinge of "Hindenburgism" with which the Army is tainted—excepting Dominion forces, wherein the negligible gulf between officers and men is easily bridged.

There will always, however, be a sneaking regard in the hearts of the few Normans who rested there; for Houvin. It was there that men could sleep far from the haunting spectre of anticipated death or devastation: there, too, life could be enjoyed to the full in the happy knowledge that no shells would pitch near by, no machine-gun turn its whining trail of bullets across your path. And it was at first difficult to realise that danger to limb was past, that movement to and fro was free from the hovering shrapnel that had so long dogged their steps and penetrated the mind with its presence until accepted as an everyday visitation such as the sun.

Parcels and mail arrived with a glad regularity. There is no more pregnant a "reviver" of downheartedness than letters from the old people, nor is anything more liable to inspire the "pip" than the absence of such personal touches with familiar scenes. Papers can never replace the badly penned and still more badly worded missives despatched from some humble cottage. Those two pages of scrawled information go far nearer to the receiver's heart than twenty columns of polished well written print. The letter is almost a living link with all that in which he has the strongest interest ... he is far more delighted at the news of Tilly's overthrow of Jim for Jack than a mere possible fall of the British Cabinet which might be pending.

"Besides," Stumpy pointed out with unconscious irony, "you opens a paper an' you knows there ain't nothin' in it, while the ole woman might 'ave put ten bob in yer letter."

Tommy has never sufficient a supply of cash. Everywhere a few miles behind the Line a canteen or Y.M.C.A. had been pushed forward and in these places the five francs a lad receives about once a fortnight does not go very far or last long. Nor does its purchasing value cover more than a meagre supply of such commodities as cake, chocolate, tobacco and beer. With regard to the latter, stress must be laid on the fact that Tommy is far less often in a state of drunkenness than the average civilian and that he is far more prone to derive humour out of it than to drink it.

CHAPTER 10

December-January, 1918—
Flers-Le Parcq-Verchocq

Snow had fallen and sprinkled the countryside with a semi-transparent white mantle. Roads due to freezing o' nights were hard and slippery, making the going for men labouring beneath the burden of full pack irksome and heavy. The Normans had no eyes for the countryside (there is no beauty in the finest masterpieces of Nature if physical conditions are not in harmony) but had the surface before them fixedly under focus in the interest of the neck's safety.

Eighteen or so kilos (approximately 11¼ miles) over the long straight levels common to France and which, although of course the shortest route between two points is viewed by the marching columns as far longer than it actually is because of the distant visibility. And Tommy would prefer a more winding journey even if the distance covered is greater.

The night's rest at Flers in the midst of heavy falls of snow put the wind up the men at the knowledge of a longer march on the morrow, but the alarm was false and a trek of four kilos materialised—hard going the whole way—to Le Parcq, a town situated on the top of a hill, the discovery of a short cut causing the break from schedule. The "cut" was made up a steep incline that proved a severe obstacle to the wildly struggling horses of transport wagons on the vile surface. Several lorries with the all-essential stores, blankets, etc., found the "glass" road utterly impassable.

This unfortunate set-back reacted on the men, who, because of the blanket shortage were doomed to but *one* per man throughout the winter night of fierce cold, against which the shivering, suffering lads had as protection billets without roofs and in some instances with mere relics of sides. The pain was acute, sleep difficult. Some unable to withstand

71

the torture paced up and down the whole night through, banging arms heavily across bodies to stimulate some semblance of warmth.

At the first indications of dawn they were started on what proved to be one of the longest marches in their experience. The weather was harsher than on any of the preceding days and the frozen snow surface of the roads presented in itself a factor that materially magnified the heavy labouring beneath full pack, arduous to a degree under the easiest of conditions. Before mid-day the constant vigilance and care necessary if a hard fall was to be avoided began to tell on the nerves, irritability forced its grip, and they glared savagely at one another at every sideslip—inevitable in a long trek over such roads.

After twenty or so kilos had been reeled off physical exhaustion invaded man after man, growling ceased, heads bent forward and the eyes watched unseeing the heels of the man ahead. Mechanical rigidity of monotonous, torturous march again held sway, the old dryness of tongue and aching of burning feet grew more and more acute at each heavy step forward.

An hour passed in painful silence, and another, but ever onward along the long trail of miles—left, right, left. At each step you muttered it softly—left right—or counted them one by one until the mind rambled on confused in tens of thousands. A stage had been attained when one felt nothing, knew nothing, but just the unending chorus of padding feet guided by the mere instinct of a mind in a condition of peculiar coma. The ten minute halts were taken at each hour with no comment. Men threw themselves prone on the road, closed eyes, stood up unthinking at the order and fell again into the harsh rigidity of movement.

Just before dusk the "machine" halted at Verchocq, after a march of thirty-three kilos. They were tired, worn, hungry....

No lorries or cookers turned up that night!

Followed that abrupt revival of spirits that cannot but remain a psychological mystery. No cookers—no grub. They threw aside without an effort complete exhaustion, the outcome of an entire day's strenuous bodily exertion, sallied forth with remarkable sangfroid and certainty in Verchocq, there conversing with the inhabitants, made themselves thoroughly at home and gratefully partook of the hot fare hospitably provided them—the fierce inroads upon food that only the utterly famished can readily appreciate, and which indelibly impressed upon the intellect of their hosts a certainty that British troops could never have their appetite satiated.

They returned to billets in varying moods and conditions, one or two ignoring a straight walk and zigzagging an uncertain course across the roads. Stumpy, who had received a generous welcome from a misguided patriot, sat down with smug complacency, holding one hand lovingly over an abdomen over-filled with good fare.

"Weren't 'alf orl right," he said "lawd, wot with five eggs an' 'am an' bread; but there weren't any beer, only," with a shudder, "a 'ome-made lemonade."

"Yus," Duquemin agreed, "dam good-hic-sort these French people. Fine lil' daughter wi' blue-hic-eyes. 'Eld my 'and, and she *hic*-said was brave-*hic* soldier. Ver' proud ... 'allo wot-hic-doing'."

A lad was kneeling in his corner, hands clasped in prayer. (He did so night after night unmolested.) The crowd watched curiously—but had anyone dare to scoff they, as Mahieu said, "would a' knocked the b— scoffer's 'ead orf."

Strange ingrained instinctive assertion of fair play predominant in the attitude of those wild, uncouth mortals. Few of them had thought of outward expression of God—a fierce resentment world galvanise into life at the slightest sneer upon the unprotected back of those who *had* the pluck. From his couch in a solitary blanket the agnostic grunted. "Fetish," he observed quietly, "the warrior appealing to his oracle of Delphi like a savage to his moon. Passing gods of a passing generation...."

"Yesh," Duquemin agreed sagely. "Passin' gen'ral rashon—no rashon-hic-pore-Guernseys. Oonly wot people gi'...."

The friendship originated during the Normans' first night at Vorchocq with the French grew as the days progressed, accentuated by the Norman knowledge of the people's mother-tongue.

They made the utmost of their time, lived life to the very full, inspired by the knowledge that the draft of four hundred Staffords and two hundred or so Guernseymen (the ten per cent. who had not participated at Cambrai) who were to become absorbed into the Ten Hundred were auguries of an approaching further acquaintance with the Front Line.

Christmas Day provided an ample fare in addition to the ordinary rations, small parties engaging rooms in estaminets and farms, purchasing the very limit of eatables obtainable with what financial lengths were at their disposal, obtained bottles of port and gave vent to an unbounded vein of hilarious humour and uproarious chorus in celebration of a Christmas that many knew would be their last.

In a quiet room four of the ascetic rankers (Clarke, Martel, Lomar and White) passed an evening that will long remain a pleasant memory, tempered with pain for the one who soon afterwards paid the Supreme Sacrifice.

Everywhere uproar was rampant. Light, laughter, and good cheer maintained undisputed sway upon all. Rose-cheeked daughters of France were toasted again and again, taken into muscular arms and kissed times without number.

The old marching rallies of the Ten Hundred were roared out from every tiny house ablaze with light, echoed out into the inscrutable pall of black and wafted far away into the shadows.

And they toasted the "Old Battalion," the warriors who were lying in the damp Masnières soil; the Future; and God's own Isle—their little motherland. It hurt, how it hurt! How the tiny green island rose mistily before the eyes in all its sun-bathed romance and mystery! How the sweet aroma of its gold, furze-crowned cliffs, the laughter of blue waters, the lowing of cattle, came flooding with glad memories on the mind ... and *you* may not ever again scent that furze or glimpse those waters!

They laughed memory back into its dim past. *what* of the future? Live only for the present!

Bunny was happy. Reclining gracefully in the gutter he sang a jumbled lullaby of melodies.

There's maggots in the cheese,
You can 'ear the beggars sneeze—

He struggled manfully to his feet, fell into a helpless fit of laughter and collapsed again into the roadway with a heavy grunt. An N.C.O. found him there a few minutes later.

"'Ere," he demanded, "wot are you doin' there?"

"Doin'," Bunny chuckled helplessly: "wot think I'm doin ... plantin' daisies or diggin' for gold?"

"Look 'ere, me lad, if you're lookin' for trouble—!"

"Lookin' for trouble?—not lookin' for anything. Just 'avin' a rest by the wayside an' gazin' at stars."

"Well, get up or I'll 'old you up, an' you'll *see* 'em then."

"Or-righ'. Want, want, lil' drop toddy?"

"Got much? Pass it over."

"Ain't got none. Only asked if you *want* a-a drop...." He moved away and from far down the street his dirge carried faintly:

There's whiskers on the pork
We curl 'em with a fork—

In unhappy contract to Christmas. New Year proved to be a day of short rations, bully beef and a rehearsal of an attack in the snow. The bread ration dwindled down to Winkleian proportions.

A move up the line was pending in the near future and rumours that of all hellish sectors they were going up the Passchendaele-Ypres areas, were received with continuous outbursts of growling.

The young Staffords who had not the gruesome knowledge of Belgian desolation were satisfied with a front anywhere near the magic Ypres. They wanted to see the place where, as one of them was perpetually saying. "A couple of Blighty regiments made a bloomin' 'ell of a mess of the whole blooming' Jerry army."

There was everywhere a mutual recognition of a possible, a probable, German attack on a scale to date unparalleled. Every battalion in the Brigade was thoroughly cognisant that at some time during the next few months they would be called upon to make another Cambrai stand. There was a general feeling that he would attempt to crush the British Army at a blow, seize the Channel ports, and thus isolate what armies had escaped the first onslaught.

CHAPTER 11

December-January, 1918— Leulene-Brandhoek-Ypres

January 3.—Snow had, after three weeks on the ground beneath the hardening influence of a temperature several degrees below zero, evolved into a surface upon which a constant steady balance demanded no little skill. Marching encumbered with a full pack, clumsy Army-shod feet, one arm only free for a much hampered swing, increased the difficulties of maintaining a secure foothold.

(Full pack: A conglomeration of articles intended in normal ages to be transported by two mules, but under the influence of advanced civilisation strapped on the back of one man, in addition to a rifle, half a dozen Mills' bombs, a Lewis-gun, spade or shovel, sheet of corrugated iron, or any other article that can be somewhere hung upon him).

Weariness, fedupity, after many miles had been laboriously reeled off, was a factor in slackening vigilance on the semi-ice, many painful falls resulting—to fall with a pack produces a situation resembling a beetle on its back.

Stumpy pulled someone out of a snowdrift—then he fell into one himself, unnoticed. He caught the Battalion up at the halt.

"Oh, 'ell," he shouted indignantly, "I might a' died for all you bloomin' well cared."

"Why, wot's up?"

"Up? I fell into a bloomin' drift."

"Oh, an' wot the 'ell d'you do that for?"

"Do it for. Why, why...!" The crowd about him grinned.

"P'raps 'e saw 'is ole woman comin' along the road."

"'E saw the bloomin' captain drop a *skate* (fag-end) down an' went after it."

"That's the way 'e 'as 'is weekly wash."

"He was playin' snowballs with 'is bloomin' self."

The command to "fall in" dropped the curtain.

In the grey of dusk the shadowy column marched into Leulene.

The Ten Hundred, after an eleven days' "rest" in the icy grip of a winter's wind that clung to Leulene unabating throughout the period, marched away and entrained upon their first portion of journey front-linewards.

Cattle-trucks provide ample novelty, aroma and draughts. Refuse covering the floor is swept by the occupants into a corner heap, but someone has to sleep on it. An open space between a sliding door can comfortably accommodate two with legs dangling over, but invariably has four or more hunched-up, jumbled khaki figures.

These trains never hurry: always twist and turn and double back half-a-dozen times in journeyings from one point to another. Jolting and jarring is unnoticed—you are past noticing anything after the first hour!

Officers have usually the luxury of railway carriages, but the private—*Privates*: Individuals who form the large proportion of a Battalion. Their salient duties embrace shining buttons, carrying up officers' rations, dodging parades, scrubbing out sergeants' and officers' mess, squad drill, guards, and C.B., picking up paper near the billets, grousing and growing thin on short rations—during spare moments they are used for fighting.

Detraining at Brandhoek, the Ten Hundred marched to Brake Camp, a rambling collection of huts built in a wood near the main road running between Poperinghe and Ypres, within a short distance of Vlamertynghe.

It was "Pop!" Unchanged, grim and grey, visited day and night by bomb and shell with the ceaseless activity of that Belgian area. A battalion of Worcesters, whom the Normans were relieving, painted a merry picture of the sodden sector.

"Fritz ain't 'alf playin' 'ell wi' the front line. Washed out two blasted regiments in less than a week...."

"No bloomm' trenches up there. Only shell 'oles an' hundreds of bodies. Ration parties can't get up wi' the grub...."

"Jerry shells like 'ell orl night an' sends over gas in shells and cloud orl day. Three 'undred casualties last week an' I 'eard that alf of 'em kicked the bucket...."

"Old Jerry 'as a million troops from Russia waitin' to come over next month for his offensive...."

"Yus, Sir Daggie 'Aig sez 'e must sacrifice 'is First Lines. An', wots more, yer up to the neck in water...."

The Normans slept that night haunted by nightmare visitations created by minds pervaded with strong "windupity." Stumpy succumbed to a. fit of depression from which nothing could rouse him. Evans (a Stafford) gave him a fag.

"Cheer up," he said.

"Can't? Bloomin' water up to yer neck an' they don't issue lifebelts an' I can't swim."

"Garn. That's only wot they *sez*."

"Gas an' shells an' troops."

"Only bloomin' rumours."

"An' no ration parties can got up—oh gawd!"

"Wot about it?"

"No ration parties means no grub an' *no* rum. Wot a pore Tommy 'as got ter put up with."

The following day marching through Ypres they moved further up the Line to a camp situated near St. Jean and from whence they would make their final preparations and march towards the duck-board (a series of boards resembling actual duck-boards and raised to a height above the ground varying in accordance to the depth of water) track winding up the wasted shell-torn soil to the communication trenches.

The "atmosphere" of the place was painfully reminiscent to the survivors from the previous September of the nerve-wrecking task that had been their unfortunate lot during that Baptism of Fire. The grim devastation of the flat, water-covered countryside enforced upon the spirits something of its own desolation. Everywhere the gaunt, shell-shattered trees, through which o' nights the incessant red glow eastward penetrated just as it had four months before. Day and night the perpetual roar of artillery, the heavy shock of falling bombs, the familiar *kr-ump!*

And the knowledge that the brief security of life had passed. Again, already, none knew who might not glimpse the dawn; again the hell-hot shrapnel and the writhing human flesh. Tomorrow that arm may be a shattered, jagged hanging "thing" ... how firm, fine, and white it looks: smooth, strong....

You look curiously along the line of adjacent faces. Can *all* come through—impossible. Who will go under first ... will it be *you*? Wonder what it is like to die? Men had often fallen limply near by, a small round hole in the forehead and a trickle of blood. They seemed calm enough ... wonder where they went ... did they *know* they were dead? Do you feel the bullet whistling through your brain ... do you have one last lightning thought cut short, "This is Death!"...?

Anyhow, what of it ... others have done it. If they could, you could!

Before going up into the icy-cold of water-logged semi-trenches the feet were treated with special attention to counteract the action of continual wet and frost upon the flesh. If the utmost care is not taken, and the dreaded "trench feet" fastens its fierce grip upon the victim, there lies before him many weeks of agony in hospital, haunted daily by a chance of losing one or both feet. All this without the glad consolation of a *wound*!

Washed in warm water, the feet are greased and powdered and new socks placed carefully over before setting out on the trudge Linewards.

Trench equipment is issued, two days' rations served out, and a start is made in the night. Stumpy lost his "grub" by misadventure, but found somebody else's, withstood a fierce argument for ten minutes and finally pacified his opponent by "finding" still another issue.

Hoarse orders sent men probing about for their rifles and assortment of equipment.

The Ten Hundred filed out.

CHAPTER 12

Passchendaele Sector

Eyes gazing eastward at the rising and falling Verey Lights in Jerry's lines, the Ten Hundred trudged wearily along a sodden plank "road" winding into a stretch of muddy track strewn on all sides with the gruesome conglomeration of war's jetsam.

The way had to be carefully chosen past shell-holes full of water, with here and there a slowly twirling body, a white face shining hideously in the damp night air. To the south a wavering mass of searchlights flitted over the sky. Archie guns were raising a fierce distant clamour, the white puffs from their bursting shrapnel showing like gigantic snowballs in the glare, but no trace of the Fritz airmen was visible. A series of violent concussions and the faint high-up throb of aero engines were the only indications of his gambols.

Then silent filing along a poor system of filthy trenches ... the other battalion was relieving. Posting of men, reliefs....

To stand there in the night, suffering acutely from the cold, unmoving, staring fascinated across the little stretch of desolation between the lines and to watch fanciful shadows until the mind falls prey to apprehensive imagination construing the posts and wiring into great fantastic grey-cloaked figures. Then at the turn of the head—*what* is that? In one frenzied movement the rifle is levelled across the parapet, first pressure of the trigger taken and the shadowy bulk watched. Five long minutes of intense scrutiny—it *moved*, or was it mere fancy? There again—*crack!!* And the figure has not fallen ... so through the darkness, until day reveals a shrivelled form tangled up on the wire where it died days ago.

Parts of the area were simply connected shell-holes, outposts, the occupants of which might for hours at a stretch be completely isolated from the remainder of their battalion, and, receiving no visit from anyone, have not the merest inkling of what was going on outside of what lies before their own limited vision.

The failure of water supply reaching these outposts increased an already severe existence. Someone would go "over the top," crawl to and fill water-bottles up at the nearest shell-hole. A body or limb might be at the bottom—who cares! The water is rank, putrid, evil-smelling; but the fierce, mad craving for drink is not to be denied.

A shell found one of the small advanced posts, killed a few outright and gashed a long tear into the abdomen of the one survivor. He languished there alone with the dead for eight hours—they had been "lost." He was found, removed, died before reaching a Casualty Clearing Station. Inexorable law of Chance.

Fritz sent over gas shells night and day, hampering rationing parties, and enforcing prolonged agony inside the hot respirators. Gas, heavier than air, hangs low over the ground, follows inundations up and down, and slinks across water: hanging for days over damp soil, and permeating water with a sickly colour—an obvious danger to troops drinking this liquid.

Where the country was flooded duck-boards were raised to a height sufficient to stand above the water and presented at night (all movements are generally done at nightfall) an alluring task of maintaining balance on a narrow planking (couple of feat or so) adorned with no handrails or supports and invisible five feet away. When Fritz sends over gas and respirators have to be donned during the intricate negotiation of this "pathway"—!

Clarke and Bennet, moving gingerly beneath two heavy ration issues, paused abruptly to duck to a whining shell. The latter slipped, fell off into the miniature ocean, clambered out.

"Oh, 'ell, bloomin' bread too—*look out!*"

"That's the second dud."

"Yes, must be gas." Respirators on they were unable to peer a foot either way, sat down uncomfortably on the boards and waited for the attack to move away. But when they did stand up and gazed about them ... *which way was which?*

The absence in places of any line or wiring (posts would not stand up in the watery soil) permitted men o' nights to wander unawares towards the Fritz trenches. A crack, a fall—for weeks the body would lie outside the enemy lines until it rotted and fell apart. And someone was posted "Missing."

Trench feet began to find its victims among the young Staffords—

they trekked away in agony, but withal glad to get out of it. With the puzzling rapidity of trench casualties the daily roll increased without anyone quite grasping how or when this or that man went. He would be with you this morning, tomorrow you would miss him; inquire and learn that he had stopped a Blighty.

Evans, an adherent of the occult, vowed that he had been visited by some eternal being of the spirit world. Stumpy was profoundly interested.

"Wot'd 'e say?"

"Nothing much. Only that somethin' would portend for me to-morrow."

"Oh, did 'e want a drink?"

"Course not."

"If 'e 'ad asked you for your rum ration, would you," anxiously, "'ave given it to 'im."

"Couldn't: 'adn't any left."

"Wot woz 'e like?"

"Tall, shadowy."

"An' you really believes it?"

"Yus. I 'ave proof—"

"I see. I, I s'pose 'e could give you anything you asked 'im for?"

"Within reason."

"Then," whispered ironically, "ask 'im next time to give me a soft Blighty an' a drop of toddy, an', oh, some bloomin' fags."

"Can't be done, for something will 'appen to me tomorrow."

He was wrong; decided that the spook had altered for his own good reasons the daily course of his life and eagerly awaited a visit that never materialised. Stumpy was disgusted.

"All me eye. I know it wasn't a bloomin' spook when I 'eard 'e 'adn't asked for a drink. Wot on earth would anyone visit these yere bloomin' trenches for unless he smelt rum?"

"You don't understand."

"No, an' bloomin' well don't want to. A spook wot rejoins 'is ole friends on earth an' don't even offer 'em a drink is unnatural—that's wot I say."

The large, dry and roomy dug-out beloved by the armchair artist, very, very rarely offers its cosy hospitality to the warrior dwelling in the Front Line—even if there is anything bearing a faint resemblance to such an elaboration it is immediately seized by Company Headquarters. The inter-connecting series of holes occupied by the

Normans and flattered with the term "trenches" had cut here and there into the wet soil a number of side excavations of smart proportions that served the purpose of shelter from the elements and shells alike—a heavy barrage from a pea-shooter would have blown in the muddy roofs of these water-logged death traps.

To reach the rear lines movement could only be made *on the top* and fully exposed to enemy snipers, who, suffering badly from forced inactivity and ennui, delighted to exercise their shooting powers by a few minutes' pleasant concentration upon your helpless figure.

Mud and water, upon which floated an interesting conglomeration of filthy rubbish, flowed saucily around your ankles, sometimes your knees, and when you fell off a high duckboard, your neck.

The humour of it—afterwards! The acute misery and suffering of those long, long nights standing in water; cold, hungry and weary. Body aching from the fierce winter's blast and the fingers gone stiff, immovable, almost unfeeling ... with no hope for the future, but always the ceaseless watch and wait until the great Peace of Death overtakes the tired body and a troubled soul leaves its burden to be carried on by those who follow after.

Rain lashed stinging into the face, dripping in rivulets from off the steel helmet and forcing its way into the neck ... the shrieking of an unnerving wind ... the blast of mighty shell ... the gas ... death was *not* the worst alternative. Fritz played heavily on the back areas; we returned shell for shell, but no infantry action took place on either side during the eight days of Norman occupation. The enemy was concentrating his man-power for a Push with the opening of finer days, and we did not have an excess of men to waste after the heavy toll of the Cambrai stunt.

The Ten Hundred were relieved for a brief rest.

CHAPTER 13

Passchendaele Sector—
Poperinghe-Steenvoorde-Brandhoek

The Ten Hundred had revelled in the luxury of a hot bath. "Casey," who had found and hurriedly slipped into his trouser pocket a full packet of "fags" inadvertently left behind by some individual with an unbalanced mind, portrayed his bare arm for general admiration of the four small scars thereon.

"Waccinated," he said, "by good ole Kinnersley." (Dr.—Captain Kinnersley, undoubtedly the one man who held the softest corner in the hearts of all the old Normans, and whose friendly hand-shakes as from man to man were never forgotten by the "boys" of the original 1st Battalion).

"Wots the good?" Le Page demanded.

"Good—wot a question. Why, it stops fever, an' smallpox, an' almost everythin'."

"Any good fer toothache?" The crowd chuckled noisily.

"Would it stop a clock?"

"Any good for a bloomin' non-stop thirst?"

"P'raps it might stop the war?"

"Ever tried it on yer ole woman's tongue, Casey?—but it wouldn't stop that!"

They were interrupted by a command from the Company Officer to "get a move on." Company Officer controls a Company. Main functions to dole out pay (when he's not stopping it), C.B., and rum.

C.B. (Confined to Barracks) and similar punishments are usually granted you by the genial administrator as an adequate reward for such crimes as too little razor, too much beer, too weak a polish, or too strong a language, late on fatigue or early *off* it....

Some men are always in trouble, but provided with a programme of glib excuses and prepared at a moment's notice to call witnesses (false), always escape punishment. Some do not care if punished or not and who boast that they had full value for their "two days C.B." Heaume had a cute dodge of replying to an officer's angry expostulation that he (Heaume) had already been "up" twenty times with: "No, sir,—only sixteen so far."

Seven or eight days at Brake Camp were followed by a week at English Camp, from whence working parties daily moved up the Line by rail to the vicinity of Merrythought Station. The Ten Hundred were put through the mill as never before. "Out fer a rest," a Stafford summed up, "be 'anged fer a yarn ... called the last place Brake ... breaking us in fer this."

Poperinghe made up for it. A week without one Jerry aeroplane dropping an experimental bomb or two, without the unpleasant company of Jerry shells and free from apprehensive hours of uncertainty following a gas alarm from forward areas in an unfavourable wind.

To be able to purchase from the inhabitants almost every conceivable necessity dear to the heart of the soldier, to mingle freely with "civvies," to walk on hard, firm roads, theatres, cinemas, and to mingle nightly with other regiments compensated somewhat for what had passed.

They were shyly proud of their Cambrai record, said little of their deeds before other men, but withal treasured up every meagre speech of candid appreciation emanating spontaneously from those who had heard of, but hitherto had not met the 1st Royal Guernsey. Stumpy, assisted by his diminutive Middlesex pal, unofficially appointed himself an authority on Normans and their place in European history.

"It was like this yere," he informed a crowd of Essex in the Church Army Canteen one quiet evening, "we 'elped to make a 'ell of a mess of England an' the chap wot we fought for made us, us—"

"Granted you democratic self-government."

"Eh, yes, wot you said."

"But you don't play games—football, cricket—in Guernsey."

"Why don't we?'

"You 'aven't any room ... you'd kick the ball over the side into the sea." The Englishmen grinned.

"Wot do they wear—clothes or just a belt?"

"Don't s'pose they eat each other?"

"Wonder if any of 'em's black?"

"Wot do they live in—wigwams or caves?"

Stumpy, conscious of somehow saying the wrong thing and hurt by the shower of friendly sarcasm, shrugged his shoulders.

"Orl right," he said, "take the bloomin' advantage of the tiny isle—any'ow we 'ad the guts to come out yere."

"That's right, kid," someone offered him a fag, "you were a democracy, a free country, long before England was *England* at all, before the British Empire was dreamed of. You were the first elements of that Empire...."

"'Ere," said Stumpy, grinning with delight, "'ave a bloomin' drink."

"Your Battalion saved a whole Division at Cambrai—."

"Ave a bloomin' nother!"

Even during this "rest" in Pop., working parties were daily sent up on missions varying in detail but never in hardship or risk. They groused and growled, maintained that their physical condition was becoming worn down by the excess of work, insisted angrily that a rest should be a *rest* and not a camouflaged existence of heavy fatigues, pointed out that if Jerry came over he would find them too utterly washed out to jab a bayonet into an ounce of butter, much less a man, and finally demanded in disgust "if they were the only available Battalion in the Army and whether they had to clean up the whole bloomin' Front?"

Once within the hospitable walls of Talbot House (can any Tommy ever look back upon that oasis in war's grim desert without pangs of pleasant memories) and ensconced deep down in armchairs they forget working parties and fatigues.

From there they penned their difficult missives home-bound, there they read and re-read what few lines of intimate information could be eagerly gleaned from those brief treasured letters from home over the waters to them.

There was something almost tragic in the downcast look of those who turned their day's mail aimlessly over with anxious hands and at last shamefacedly requested some sunny-natured fellow to read out what was writ thereon. The awful reaping of ignorance, the great void of their apathetic existence!

What pregnant apprehension of drawing blank pervaded the mind as the eye expectantly watched the fast dwindling mail in the hands of the N.C.O. bawling out each name. The exhilarating thrill of glad delight with which you realised *your* name and number had been called almost at the end of the file ... the sense of lonely desolation when there has been nothing for two days ... back to that torn copy of a magazine that has been read, re-read, and re-read again and again. But you can't settle down. They have forgotten you. You don't mind the hell of existence out here, but their letter was due yesterday and now—"Bah!" bitterly, "let them bloomin' well forget."

The Ten Hundred moved into Steenvoorde and found themselves entangled in the intricacies of rehearsals for, and then later actual parade of Ceremonial Reviews. Here also they had the opportunity of indulging in that salient portion of training that appealed to them as nothing else—"firing." Undamaged by shell, cosy, they would have appreciated a lengthy spell with little to do, but rumours of an avalanche of troops that were manoeuvring behind the enemy lines became the predominant topic of discussion and lead to preparations for further movements.

All material (by ceaseless working parties) had been withdrawn

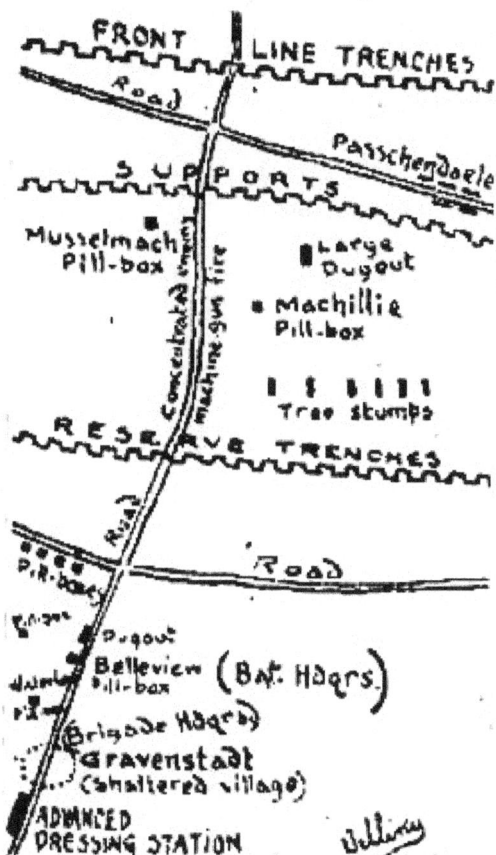

from forward areas. Troops moving out to rest were maintained at points within a few miles of the Line, and could be rushed up without appreciable delay into any gap that Jerry might by pure weight of numbers force in the British lines—nothing was left to chance.

It was pointed out that he would never attempt Flanders mud after the British experience in the Passchendaele-Poelcapelle stunts of September-October, 1917. This was countered by that pivot of sentimental strategy—Ypres. He wanted it—therefore....

He would not *get it*, anyhow!

In the midst of all these conflicting rumours and views the Normans marched to Godewaersvelde and entrained there for a return to Brandhoek. At Red Rose Camp they prepared for another lengthy period in the Line, about the second week in March moved up to another camp in a shelled area.

Jerry's offensive was expected at any moment; everybody was nervy: and each Battalion as it came out of the Line thanked its lucky stars that they had escaped the first onslaught. To even the ignorant strategist it was patent that either side could, by a preconceived attack, penetrate a mile or so into any chosen sector of a few miles frontage: but such a salient had little absolute value in a scheme of operations having the turning or breaking of a portion of front as objectives. A break had to be made of twenty or thirty miles and ten or twelve deep, at a stroke, otherwise with the wonderful elasticity of modern warfare the smashed-in line would reform, the gap be lost temporarily and by slight withdrawal of flanks the entire front straighten out and become once more a concrete whole.

Jerry knew it—and we knew he knew it.

CHAPTER 14

March-April, 1918—In the Line

California Camp, the Normans' jumping off point for their *in* and *out* occupation of the trenches and working parties when not in the former, was composed of a collection of tiny huts constructed on similar lines to the Nissen. The attractions peculiar to this obnoxious assortment of pygmy habitations were two: could not lie down straight in them, absolutely impossible to stand up. Circular of roof, mode of entrance was an enforced elegant attitude on hands and knees wherein a decided advantage could be derived by going in lobster-wise—backwards, for there was *not* an ample space in which to turn about.

Jerry artillery had fitful moods of strafing. Days of wild "searching" with a disgusting series of violent heavies bursting in all directions, blowing out candles with the concussion and in the darkness bringing about language-provoking situations that culminated in clumsy searches for matches ... light would reveal your watery rice careering smugly about in a boot and half a dozen fags floating sadly in the remnant of your mess tin of tea!

Bitter cold of night increased. Boots, however soft and pliable when taken off, however well oiled, would be frozen hard and stiff in the morning as if cut in steel. To force these essential protections on called for painful, struggling efforts.... The only remedy was to sleep with the boots next the body. Placing beneath a pillow was fatuously inadequate.

They went into the line on a frontage beyond the actual Passchendaele village and on the far side of the ridge looking down on Jerry trenches. Watery mud again everywhere ... a further protection of sandbags around the legs was not a success; trench feet became more and more prevalent and the germs of trench fever placed Martel, Robin and a long roll on the casualty list.

Eight days of it, followed by arduous fatigues and working parties in the reserve lines. Trenches upon trenches in relays were with difficulty cut into a spongy soil, having apparently one fixed intention, e.g., to clog on to the spade in gummy lumps. Redoubts were constructed under directions from R.E.'s and a series of strong points run up at brief intervals.

When Jerry decided to come over he would have an ample reception. The weather had developed a finer, milder tone, enabling the occupants of enemy observation balloons to peer down on the mass of men engaged in rapid construction of several reserve lines of defence. At times the fit would take him to play on these exposed areas with his artillery, raining on the troops a brief fierce barrage, blowing men, horses and wagons to fragments in all directions, and playing mad havoc amongst partially-completed earthworks ... but the work went on.

Another eight days in! Night raids, patrols—casualties. Jerry came over once in the early morning—he went back!

A party of R.E.'s moving up from the south-'ard brought with them tidings of what had occurred near St. Quentin.

"Jerry started 'is little game. Came over in thousands," The speaker was overwhelmed with eager inquiries.

"Anythin' doin'?", "Did we wash 'im out?", "Wot 'appened?"

"One at a time. Smashed in our line on a fifty mile front."

"*Wot!*" shouted in chorus.

"Yus. St. Quentin fallen. Fifth Army fair smashed up."

"Good Gawd!"

"Ten miles into our lines."

"Oh, 'ell!"

"Took thirty thousand prisoners—Gawd knows 'ow many guns."

"*Wot!*"

"Thousands of casualties."

"And 'ave we stopped 'im?"

"No—still fallin' back."

Pessimism, something akin to consternation, found a hold upon the mental outlook of the troops in the sector. They had held an extraordinary unshakeable faith in the might of the Army, in its absolute certainty of holding impregnable what had been theirs from 1916, and upon which all enemy attempts had realised no concrete success.

And now, at one mighty knock-out blow, the Army was in retreat on a fifty mile front!

They glanced back upon Ypres. He would try for it ... take it? Day after day the black budget of "falling back", "prisoners", "using up our man-power," put the wind up them to such an extent that they began to curse at their own impotency and helplessness; to fret angrily at a forced comparative inactivity.

Why were they kept up there while "nothing was doing"? Why were they not sent south to give a hand to the lads who were daily fighting a stubborn retreat against avalanches of German reserves?

The Passchendaele sector remained unusually quiet; little strafing occurred from either artillery, with the exception of a sunset entertainment organised daily for the benefit of ration parties and reliefs.

Aeroplanes, after prolonged reconnaissances far into Jerry's territory, returned and the observers reported no movement or massing of enemy troops, guns or transport were taking place on a scale beyond the customary. No advance upon Ypres was at the moment anticipated unless he still farther stretched out an already extended, far-flung battle zone.

The working parties put their backs into the work with every intention of making a line upon which some thousands of Huns would be rendered casualties before it capitulated. Jerry, watching them do it, with ironical humour left them alone as if their labour were in vain, and long before the trenches would be required the British Army would be cut in two. Perhaps!

Fritz adopted a nasty habit in the form of lobbing over from fifteen miles away a new type of heavy shell, apparently under experimental observation. One fell among the Guernsey cookers, tearing a chunk cut of Sergt. Le Lacheur (he had been waiting for a Blighty for months), wounding several and mauling a few into fearsome masses of red flesh.

Grouser—he had not been with the Battalion long—found vent for his feelings. "Ain't got any blarsted sense, them Germans aint. War—it ain't war to smash up the bloomin' cookers ... 'ow the 'ell does 'e think we'll do about grub now?"

"Complain. Grouser, ole son, to the C.O." (C.O.: Commanding Officer—the colonel.—Draws the best paying winner in the Battalion Stakes and also the softest job). He was let in for a baiting.

"Send Jerry a bar of chocolate in exchange for a new cooker."

"Ask 'em to confer the O.B.E. on the Jerry wot fired the shell."

"You needn't worry about the grub. Grouser—you can live on nuts."

"Plenty of hay with the transport."

"Oh," Grouser turned abruptly, "plenty of hay.... You found yer bloomin' natural fodder, eh! Aye, ye're every bit such a donkey as ye look."

"Look 'ere, wot d'you take me for?"

"Take you for? Wouldn't take you fer a bloomin' gift. We used to have one like you with our organ—'ad it on a chain."

The Ten Hundred prepared after a last night in the line to move back during the first week in April for the long rest upon which their anticipations had been longingly concentrated for weeks.

No Battalion moved more than a few miles behind the sectors owing to the uncertainty of future enemy developments. His line of attack had been lengthened from both original flanks until at the lull in his scheme of offensive a length of over seventy miles had been attained.

He was preparing for a second wild onslaught, again to the far south of Passchendaele ... of the result everyone felt a little uncertain. It was obvious that sooner or later he would attempt a headlong rush upon those lines of communication with the Home Country—Channel Ports—so vital a factor in the efficient maintenance of the B.E.F.

The Normans came out. D Company was sent on in the direction of Proven, attained within a kilo of the town and was intercepted by a despatch rider, who carried with him orders for their immediate return. A stir of apprehensive uncertainty spread through the ranks. What had happened? Surely they were not going to be rushed into the line somewhere ... they had only just come out.

They turned, encountered the Battalion at Brandhoek. A fleet of lorries was awaiting them.

Something was *on*.

A thunderstorm turned its lashing rain upon their unprotected forms, drenched them utterly and damped their spirits. A sense of some indefinable presentiment of future dimmer crept over the mind, that subtle consciousness of approaching death forced its black pessimism upon their thoughts. They watched the heavy grey clouds scuttling overhead, watched the rain dropping from off each man's steel helmet, and gazed across the long desolate stretch of watery earth, tangled debris and shattered cottages.

Shivering with the cold, wet, hungry and weary. An hour before, marching elated in the knowledge of a few days' freedom from the haunting knowledge of Life's uncertainty—now they were in for something they all pregnantly felt would involve them in a slaughter that might place Finis to the Battalion. The Cambrai survivors stared sadly into the closing gloom ... they had gone through Rues Vertes—*could* their luck hold twice!

The lorries moved away ... the Norman Ten Hundred went out again to hang-on or fall, to uphold the traditions dearly bought by those who had gone over the Divide a few months before.

If they could *do it* then, they could do it *now*.

CHAPTER 15

April 10-14, 1918—Doulieu-Estaires

The Ten Hundred slept in their lorries at Berquin before moving into billets. No sign of enemy activity presented itself apart from the incessant rumble of distant guns. A Jerry 'plane came over on reconnaissance, taking little precaution and not flying high. They had unpleasant recollections of enemy 'planes, turned their rifles on him, and between C and D Companies brought him down—they took the occupants prisoners.

At five o'clock received orders to move up in the direction of Doulieu in reserve. They dug in with the inadequate implement carried in all equipment, accompanied only by an unnatural quiet. No troops were falling back on them, no hurried retreat or artillery, and no fierce strafing from enemy guns.

Throughout the night they stared far away into the East watching for the enemy who was coming. The silence was still undisturbed, they waited with fast-beating pulse for the long rows of onward, sweeping grey.... Dawn! And with it orders to move forward to Doulieu itself and there fill in the gap.

Almost into the objective before they saw him. Grey-coated forms swarmed for miles in relay upon relay of ever-increasing rows, advanced with deadly certainty, and supported by an astonishing mass of machine-guns.

The grim old spirit came to the fore. They rained in on the approaching waves a mad fire from smoking rifles and Lewis guns. His pace slackened not one jot ... again the Normans pumped in the lead until the hands blistered from hot rifles. Futile! They had not the men to stop one-tenth of the foe moving in thousands over fields and hedges upon them. Teeth clenched in agony. "Curse you," they sobbed, "curse your numbers...."

His machine-guns whined over into their ranks ten or twelve thousand rounds a minute along the frontage. Men fell in huddled heaps across one another. The machine-gun barrage swept backwards and forwards over the first and second lines, sweeping and intercrossing in one mighty net ... the Normans were ordered to fall back, make liaison with battalion relieving on either flank and dig in on a new line.

Again through the night they watched the pall before them, and again Jerry made no sign. Orders were given just after daybreak for a further retirement ... they marched back four or five kilos with heavy hearts. Why not have fought to a standstill where they had first sighted him? They shrugged shoulders wearily, and turned to the task of digging in. He opened his machine-guns upon the thin row of khaki figures, a figure here and there fell forward upon the little spade into a grave he had prepared for himself. Two young Staffords collapsed side by side upon the turf and smiled fixedly up into the sky, six or eight holes perforating each chest.

The bullets whined and whistled everywhere, conveying to the mind a huge swarm of bees. He tried a long sweep of low shots, just skirting the tops of the semi-completed excavations ... got home every twenty yards or so, clean through the neck or forehead.

The Normans settled down, opened fire steadily and played havoc amongst the advanced enemy machine-guns. His progress stopped, the opposing lines sniped at each other. The Normans were in their element—they knew how to shoot.

"'Olding 'im up now."

"Yes. 'E can't shoot with 'is rifles."

"No—seems to 'ave all bloomin' machine-guns."

For two hours, they kept him pinned down to one position, wiped out his one brief rush and inspired within him an unholy fear or their rifles. They watched with fierce cunning the movements of fifty or so snipers and "light" machine-gunners creeping upon them under cover of long grasses ... a bloody fire was opened for ten minutes on the figures—the grass stained red. Not one returned.

A Battalion on the Norman right fell back under the weight of enemy forces, thereby exposing a Guernsey flank.... Another retirement and again a wild scramble across fields interlaced by row after row of irrigation canals conveying water in this wide net-like system over a large area from one main source of supply. To avoid the larger excavations men were wont to crowd into the roadways, make in a body

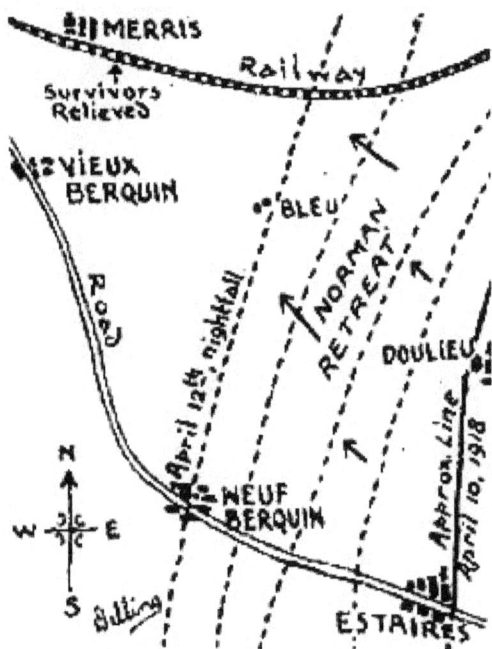

for ready gateways and openings. Upon these obvious points Jerry concentrated a continuous stream of machine-gun fire; the casualties here were heaped up hideously in small masses and the blood from one man trickled over another.

Troops from half-a-dozen regiments, scattered confusedly in all directions, moved rearwards side by side. It was almost an impossibility to rejoin Battalions—Battalions!—a mere couple of hundred men and a few officers formed what after two days of fighting constituted a Battalion. But they had to *do* the work of a full Battalion—and they *did!*

Wounded fell despairingly, gazed with appealing eyes at the lines of ever distancing khaki, placed their rifles to one side and awaited the onrushing enemy tide. Some few with what futile strength could be mustered by superhuman effort tottered and staggered uncertainly in the direction they dimly imagined their comrades had taken. One by one fell prey to exhaustion, dropped with a last frenzied sob unto the earth; some lay still and quiet, peppered by a second stream of lead. Others, writhing in agony, dazed, mad, waited the Jerry approach and picked off man after man until a bayonet thrust put *finis* to their last impotent struggles.

In secluded corners a few bled slowly undiscovered, unthought of ... there for days they remained until the bodies—lockjaw, gangrene, loss of blood—were rolled together into one great hole or perchance buried apart, and for tombstone the late owner's rifle stuck into the earth and inscribed thereon that only too frequent epitaph—an unknown British soldier!

Back, ever back! The disheartening realisation that he *cannot* be stayed for any lengthy period, that his reserves are undiminished and constantly moving up to fill the gaps made in his ranks, cast a heavy shadow of pessimism over the ragged, weary figures for ever moving westward. At lengthy intervals no sign of the grey figures anywhere met the eye, but the inevitable order to retreat was obeyed—grumbling, cursing.

"Wot the 'ell are we goin' back again for? There ain't any sign of Jerry."

"No, but 'e 'as got through too far to the south."

"Yes—an' we're moving back north-west now."

"Why?"

"Dunno. 'E's got round some'ow to the south."

An hour or undisturbed quiet. Nothing could be seen, no shells (his artillery was unable to keep pace with the rapidity of advance), no gas. Then through the silence, from nowhere it seemed, a half-spent bullet whistled and buried itself with a spiteful "phut." After a pause ... a whine, accompanied by others, falling short. In the distance his machine-gunners and advanced screen of scouts appeared ... the whining merged into a constant buzzing, men coughed furiously and bent forward, fell awkwardly ... straightened out. Here and there a khaki figure clutched fiercely at tufts of grass, writhed feverishly in one last desperate fight for breath, looked a sad farewell at their living comrades—a glance that went straight to the heart—and went their way into the warrior's hall in Valhalla.

From far down the flank a further movement rearward could be noticed spreading yard by yard until once more, weary of spirit, worn, hungry, you stood up somewhere in the stream of lead and retired.

At nightfall he would be out of view. By morning his advanced posts would be sniping at the thin khaki line. Night ... an ebony pall pierced by a score of brilliant burning houses. Fantastic, grotesque. Crimson glows upon which tired eyes rested unthinking, uncaring, the mind worn under the ceaseless repetition: *"When will we stop? Why don't they let us fight it out? God, we'd make a mess of him anyhow."*

Then someone would address no one in particular:

"Wonder 'ow many we 'ave left?"

"Gawd knows. About a 'undred an' fifty."

"See 'im toppling our lads out at Verbequie?"

"Yes. An' by that meadow gate. It makes me blood boil to think they won't let us 'ave a go at 'im."

"Ah, well. I s'pose it will be my turn tomorrow."

That is the crux of it: Your turn tomorrow? Who can tell ... what does it matter ... what is life after all? But the all-pervading ardour of youth's "Will of Life" whispers with a bitter realisation of what death really means that you *want* to live. Never before has existence been so full of future possibilities, the wish for life so poignant!

His overwhelming numerical superiority gave no evidence of slackening, his pressure on the gaping line of khaki continued unabated. No reserves, or hope of relief, were apparent. There was no alternative but to carry on day after day in continuous fighting retreat with very small numbers spread over a wide area.

Over the fields and meadows roamed farm cattle, some bleeding and running wildly about bellowing with fear. Cows moaned in agony for the dire need of milking, but who was there to do it? In the farms were sties full of half-starved pigs, grunting and groaning with hideous effect. They were turned loose to fend for themselves, ran rampant over the carefully sown ground and growing potatoes—the sad results of months of painstaking effort. Fowls fluttered and screamed with wild flapping wings, men seized the eggs and drank them down in a fierce famished hunger.

Along all the roads for miles streamed a piteous spectacle of old women, children and dogs. Before them a plaintive little barrow of belongings, on the backs of the men small red bundles tied hastily together. Wrinkled old men limped laboriously along on heavy sticks ... sometimes by the wayside a white-faced, white-haired old dame sat exhausted, crouching in fear over a poor little bundle; alone, trembling, deserted. The whine of the bullets crept nearer and troops began to pass.

"'Ere, mother, can't you get on?" Not comprehending the words but fully grasping the meaning, the unhappy old head was shaken. A passing ambulance was stopped and the frail old form gently placed in with the wounded—sometimes. There was not always an ambulance. Many a wrinkled, bent old man or woman, shrinking in fear by the roadside, were left in dire desolation to the mercy of their foe.

Some few old folks stood by their homes to the last, until the khaki rows were far across the fields away, and shot whistling about the eaves of the old thatched roof farm ... dotted here and there on their grass land a still Britisher kept them company until the Germans passed over and onward, collected the bodies, buried them.

Unshaven, tattered and unwashed, Stumpy, lamed in the left foot, potted shot after shot at each retirement, aiming at no one target, but, as he observed. "Even if I don't 'it 'im, I might puncture 'is bloomin' rum ration."

"But wot are you aimin' at?"

"Nothin'. Just 'igh in the air. Like—that there. Who knows: why it might just ketch ole Kaiser Bill in the bloomin' belly if 'e came up close 'nough."

Uncouth, uncultured, rough of manner, of speech. Good-natured, full of courage, humour. Stumpy ... short, fat and clumsy. Withal a man, a warrior. Before mid-day blood was spouting from out five vital wounds and in a few seconds faintness began to spread over him. His eyes filled with tears.

"I feels bad," he said, "can't, can't the bleedin' be stopped? I don't want to go under ... think they can get me away before Jerry comes? Things some'ow ain't over clear: everything foggy." Casey came over to him, white-faced and half-crying himself.

"You're orl right, ole pal," he said, "not bleedin' much now."

"No. But it's cloudy. D'you find it cloudy?"

"Yes. A 'ell of a mist creepin' up. Want any water?"

"No, but," with a faint grin, "got any rum?"

"'Ere you," an N.C.O. ran up and touched Casey, "Captain wants a runner. Get a move on."

"But poor ole Stumpy yere—"

"D'you 'ear wot I said. Go on, 'op it, or I'll—well, put lead in yer."

"Orl right. So long, ole pal."

"So long." Stumpy tried hard to see him through the mistiness before his eyes, "but you'll get me away before Jerry comes...." Casualty list two weeks later: "Pte.—." Missing. April 12th. He is still unheard of, forgotten. His grave is undisturbed somewhere in peaceful loneliness.

Estaires and Doulieu were several miles in the enemy lines, the Normans entangled with Staffords and Middlesex converged back past Bleu, moving as far as any one direction could be determined, approximately north-west.

There seemed to be no officers left, few over fifty Royal Guernsey ranks could be counted. Company Headquarters were no more, the scattered few had no means of access to their C.O., joined in and formed fighting blocks with mutual consent and without actual leaders, and carried on the hourly withdrawal. From out this remnant Lance-Corporal Hamel scrambled away to a dressing station, two ominous trickles of blood streaming down his legs. Winter Gregg (M.M.), too, got away in a semi-conscious condition.

One of the few trench mortar shells burst within a yard of a tall youngster. Unscathed, blackened, he turned with a piercing scream.

"God, oh my God! Where is the sun? The light 'as gone out. Someone, his voice rose to a mad shriek, 'someone come 'ere. I can't see. I'm blind, I'm blind, oh I'm blind." He threw himself on the earth and sobbed in fearful agony. They helped him to his feet, led him away, but there echoed back his remorseful wail:

"I'm blind, blind!"

That gets you. Blind! Better death....

The hours sped. Men fell with none to replace them, and in the knowledge that the enemy had fresh troops, was well supplied, and in his rear a great artillery straining forward to take part in the slaughter, aeroplanes above, the tail-end of a few decimated Battalions fought on against the hopeless odds before them. As long as a man had life in his body, rifle and shot, he used them to advantage. The next Britisher might be forty yards away or more, but until he was ordered to retire he would ... "'ang on like 'ell to that there strip."

The Staffords after three days of it, through the whole of which period they had stuck doggedly, pluckily, to their task, had dwindled down to a scattered few on the nightfall of the 15th April. Forty, perhaps fifty, completely exhausted, filthy and tattered Normans still clung about their C.O. on a frontage a few miles south of Merris. The very mechanical stupor that at last commenced to give way beneath unceasing hardship. Nature demanded sleep. Not the brief, wakeful moments snatched at intervals in the night, but sleep, long, quiet, undisturbed.

From an observation balloon high in the air above its motor trolley Jerry observers reported on the shattered remnant still holding out. He pressed home his advantage upon the tired troops ... rifles grew hot. The few Normans were again forced back.

Relief by Australians was effected near Merris. The tiny, devastated string of Normans (53) came out. But in a situation of acute urgency they were still used to construct trenches upon which withdrawal by the newly engaged Divisions could be made.

The Brigadier. G.O.C., 80th Brigade, a few weeks later bade farewell to the little force in a speech that sent a wild thrill of pride throughout the small Battalion.

In their honour the Divisional band played them on their march to a station ("Ebblingham"), from which they entrained for G.H.Q., where they were to take over duties from the H.A.C.

And thus the Passing from the Great Undertaking!

Farewell, Norman warriors who this night in Valhalla sing of mighty deeds of valour from high with the Anses.

Farewell, a sad farewell, to for ever lost echoes to ten hundred voiced raised in rallying chorus to the swing of square shoulders and the ring of manly feet.

The "old order changeth." Away from the strong fray ... free life ... laughter, glamour, song ... the Great Open ... the *men*....

Back to the little world, its little things, to *its little life*.

See ye Masnières canal a flood
And where yon green graves lay?
There Norman warriors fled to their God
Ne'er more to glimpse the day.
But writ there, first, a name in blood—
Norman Ten Hundred.

At Doulieu, the night birds flits
Across yon blue-gray water.
And in dusk ghost warriors sit—
Wraiths of a fearsome slaughter.
There too in blood the name is writ—
Norman Ten Hundred.

And thus there the battle's flame
Laid men out fast and low,
So Young Sarnia died, but Fame
Cast o'er their graves its glow,
And honours wove about the name
Norman Ten Hundred.

ALSO FROM LEONAUR
AVAILABLE IN SOFTCOVER OR HARDCOVER WITH DUST JACKET

ADVENTURES OF A YOUNG RIFLEMAN *by Johann Christian Maempel*—The Experiences of a Saxon in the French & British Armies During the Napoleonic Wars.

THE HUSSAR *by Norbert Landsheit & G. R. Gleig*—A German Cavalryman in British Service Throughout the Napoleonic Wars.

RECOLLECTIONS OF THE PENINSULA *by Moyle Sherer*—An Officer of the 34th Regiment of Foot—'The Cumberland Gentlemen'—on Campaign Against Napoleon's French Army in Spain.

MARINE OF REVOLUTION & CONSULATE *by Moreau de Jonnès*—The Recollections of a French Soldier of the Revolutionary Wars 1791-1804.

GENTLEMEN IN RED *by John Dobbs & Robert Knowles*—Two Accounts of British Infantry Officers During the Peninsular War Recollections of an Old 52nd Man by John Dobbs An Officer of Fusiliers by Robert Knowles.

CORPORAL BROWN'S CAMPAIGNS IN THE LOW COUNTRIES *by Robert Brown*—Recollections of a Coldstream Guard in the Early Campaigns Against Revolutionary France 1793-1795.

THE 7TH (QUEENS OWN) HUSSARS: Volume 2—1793-1815 *by C. R. B. Barrett*—During the Campaigns in the Low Countries & the Peninsula and Waterloo Campaigns of the Napoleonic Wars. Volume 2: 1793-1815.

THE MARENGO CAMPAIGN 1800 *by Herbert H. Sargent*—The Victory that Completed the Austrian Defeat in Italy.

DONALDSON OF THE 94TH—SCOTS BRIGADE *by Joseph Donaldson*—The Recollections of a Soldier During the Peninsula & South of France Campaigns of the Napoleonic Wars.

A CONSCRIPT FOR EMPIRE *by Philippe as told to Johann Christian Maempel*—The Experiences of a Young German Conscript During the Napoleonic Wars.

JOURNAL OF THE CAMPAIGN OF 1815 *by Alexander Cavalié Mercer*—The Experiences of an Officer of the Royal Horse Artillery During the Waterloo Campaign.

NAPOLEON'S CAMPAIGNS IN POLAND 1806-7 *by Robert Wilson*—The campaign in Poland from the Russian side of the conflict.

LEONAUR

ALSO FROM LEONAUR
AVAILABLE IN SOFTCOVER OR HARDCOVER WITH DUST JACKET

COLBORNE: A SINGULAR TALENT FOR WAR *by John Colborne*—The Napoleonic Wars Career of One of Wellington's Most Highly Valued Officers in Egypt, Holland, Italy, the Peninsula and at Waterloo.

NAPOLEON'S RUSSIAN CAMPAIGN *by Philippe Henri de Segur*—The Invasion, Battles and Retreat by an Aide-de-Camp on the Emperor's Staff.

WITH THE LIGHT DIVISION *by John H. Cooke*—The Experiences of an Officer of the 43rd Light Infantry in the Peninsula and South of France During the Napoleonic Wars.

WELLINGTON AND THE PYRENEES CAMPAIGN VOLUME I: FROM VITORIA TO THE BIDASSOA *by F. C. Beatson*—The final phase of the campaign in the Iberian Peninsula.

WELLINGTON AND THE INVASION OF FRANCE VOLUME II: THE BIDASSOA TO THE BATTLE OF THE NIVELLE *by F. C. Beatson*—The final phase of the campaign in the Iberian Peninsula.

WELLINGTON AND THE FALL OF FRANCE VOLUME III: THE GAVES AND THE BATTLE OF ORTHEZ *by F. C. Beatson*—The final phase of the campaign in the Iberian Peninsula.

NAPOLEON'S IMPERIAL GUARD: FROM MARENGO TO WATERLOO *by J. T. Headley*—The story of Napoleon's Imperial Guard and the men who commanded them.

BATTLES & SIEGES OF THE PENINSULAR WAR *by W. H. Fitchett*—Corunna, Busaco, Albuera, Ciudad Rodrigo, Badajos, Salamanca, San Sebastian & Others.

SERGEANT GUILLEMARD: THE MAN WHO SHOT NELSON? *by Robert Guillemard*—A Soldier of the Infantry of the French Army of Napoleon on Campaign Throughout Europe.

WITH THE GUARDS ACROSS THE PYRENEES *by Robert Batty*—The Experiences of a British Officer of Wellington's Army During the Battles for the Fall of Napoleonic France, 1813 .

A STAFF OFFICER IN THE PENINSULA *by E. W. Buckham*—An Officer of the British Staff Corps Cavalry During the Peninsula Campaign of the Napoleonic Wars.

THE LEIPZIG CAMPAIGN: 1813—NAPOLEON AND THE "BATTLE OF THE NATIONS" *by F. N. Maude*—Colonel Maude's analysis of Napoleon's campaign of 1813 around Leipzig.

LEONAUR

ALSO FROM LEONAUR
AVAILABLE IN SOFTCOVER OR HARDCOVER WITH DUST JACKET

CAPTAIN COIGNET *by Jean-Roch Coignet*—A Soldier of Napoleon's Imperial Guard from the Italian Campaign to Russia and Waterloo.

HUSSAR ROCCA *by Albert Jean Michel de Rocca*—A French cavalry officer's experiences of the Napoleonic Wars and his views on the Peninsular Campaigns against the Spanish, British And Guerilla Armies.

MARINES TO 95TH (RIFLES) *by Thomas Fernyhough*—The military experiences of Robert Fernyhough during the Napoleonic Wars.

LIGHT BOB *by Robert Blakeney*—The experiences of a young officer in H.M 28th & 36th regiments of the British Infantry during the Peninsular Campaign of the Napoleonic Wars 1804 - 1814.

WITH WELLINGTON'S LIGHT CAVALRY *by William Tomkinson*—The Experiences of an officer of the 16th Light Dragoons in the Peninsular and Waterloo campaigns of the Napoleonic Wars.

SERGEANT BOURGOGNE *by Adrien Bourgogne*—With Napoleon's Imperial Guard in the Russian Campaign and on the Retreat from Moscow 1812 - 13.

SURTEES OF THE 95TH (RIFLES) *by William Surtees*—A Soldier of the 95th (Rifles) in the Peninsular campaign of the Napoleonic Wars.

SWORDS OF HONOUR *by Henry Newbolt & Stanley L. Wood*—The Careers of Six Outstanding Officers from the Napoleonic Wars, the Wars for India and the American Civil War.

ENSIGN BELL IN THE PENINSULAR WAR *by George Bell*—The Experiences of a young British Soldier of the 34th Regiment 'The Cumberland Gentlemen' in the Napoleonic wars.

HUSSAR IN WINTER *by Alexander Gordon*—A British Cavalry Officer during the retreat to Corunna in the Peninsular campaign of the Napoleonic Wars.

THE COMPLEAT RIFLEMAN HARRIS *by Benjamin Harris as told to and transcribed by Captain Henry Curling, 52nd Regt. of Foot*—The adventures of a soldier of the 95th (Rifles) during the Peninsular Campaign of the Napoleonic Wars.

THE ADVENTURES OF A LIGHT DRAGOON *by George Farmer & G.R. Gleig*—A cavalryman during the Peninsular & Waterloo Campaigns, in captivity & at the siege of Bhurtpore, India.

LEONAUR

ALSO FROM LEONAUR
AVAILABLE IN SOFTCOVER OR HARDCOVER WITH DUST JACKET

LIFE IN THE ARMY OF NORTHERN VIRGINIA *by Carlton McCarthy*—The Observations of a Confederate Artilleryman of Cutshaw's Battalion During the American Civil War 1861-1865.

HISTORY OF THE CAVALRY OF THE ARMY OF THE POTOMAC *by Charles D. Rhodes*—Including Pope's Army of Virginia and the Cavalry Operations in West Virginia During the American Civil War.

CAMP-FIRE AND COTTON-FIELD *by Thomas W. Knox*—A New York Herald Correspondent's View of the American Civil War.

SERGEANT STILLWELL *by Leander Stillwell* —The Experiences of a Union Army Soldier of the 61st Illinois Infantry During the American Civil War.

STONEWALL'S CANNONEER *by Edward A. Moore*—Experiences with the Rockbridge Artillery, Confederate Army of Northern Virginia, During the American Civil War.

THE SIXTH CORPS *by George Stevens*—The Army of the Potomac, Union Army, During the American Civil War.

THE RAILROAD RAIDERS *by William Pittenger*—An Ohio Volunteers Recollections of the Andrews Raid to Disrupt the Confederate Railroad in Georgia During the American Civil War.

CITIZEN SOLDIER *by John Beatty*—An Account of the American Civil War by a Union Infantry Officer of Ohio Volunteers Who Became a Brigadier General.

COX: PERSONAL RECOLLECTIONS OF THE CIVIL WAR--VOLUME 1 *by Jacob Dolson Cox*—West Virginia, Kanawha Valley, Gauley Bridge, Cotton Mountain, South Mountain, Antietam, the Morgan Raid & the East Tennessee Campaign.

COX: PERSONAL RECOLLECTIONS OF THE CIVIL WAR--VOLUME 2 *by Jacob Dolson Cox*—Siege of Knoxville, East Tennessee, Atlanta Campaign, the Nashville Campaign & the North Carolina Campaign.

KERSHAW'S BRIGADE VOLUME 1 *by D. Augustus Dickert*—Manassas, Seven Pines, Sharpsburg (Antietam), Fredricksburg, Chancellorsville, Gettysburg, Chickamauga, Chattanooga, Fort Sanders & Bean Station.

KERSHAW'S BRIGADE VOLUME 2 *by D. Augustus Dickert*—At the wilderness, Cold Harbour, Petersburg, The Shenandoah Valley and Cedar Creek..

LEONAUR

ALSO FROM LEONAUR
AVAILABLE IN SOFTCOVER OR HARDCOVER WITH DUST JACKET

THE RELUCTANT REBEL *by William G. Stevenson*—A young Kentuckian's experiences in the Confederate Infantry & Cavalry during the American Civil War..

BOOTS AND SADDLES *by Elizabeth B. Custer*—The experiences of General Custer's Wife on the Western Plains.

FANNIE BEERS' CIVIL WAR *by Fannie A. Beers*—A Confederate Lady's Experiences of Nursing During the Campaigns & Battles of the American Civil War.

LADY SALE'S AFGHANISTAN *by Florentia Sale*—An Indomitable Victorian Lady's Account of the Retreat from Kabul During the First Afghan War.

THE TWO WARS OF MRS DUBERLY *by Frances Isabella Duberly*—An Intrepid Victorian Lady's Experience of the Crimea and Indian Mutiny.

THE REBELLIOUS DUCHESS *by Paul F. S. Dermoncourt*—The Adventures of the Duchess of Berri and Her Attempt to Overthrow French Monarchy.

LADIES OF WATERLOO *by Charlotte A. Eaton, Magdalene de Lancey & Juana Smith*—The Experiences of Three Women During the Campaign of 1815: Waterloo Days by Charlotte A. Eaton, A Week at Waterloo by Magdalene de Lancey & Juana's Story by Juana Smith.

TWO YEARS BEFORE THE MAST *by Richard Henry Dana. Jr.*—The account of one young man's experiences serving on board a sailing brig—the Penelope—bound for California, between the years1834-36.

A SAILOR OF KING GEORGE *by Frederick Hoffman*—From Midshipman to Captain—Recollections of War at Sea in the Napoleonic Age 1793-1815.

LORDS OF THE SEA *by A. T. Mahan*—Great Captains of the Royal Navy During the Age of Sail.

COGGESHALL'S VOYAGES: VOLUME 1 *by George Coggeshall*—The Recollections of an American Schooner Captain.

COGGESHALL'S VOYAGES: VOLUME 2 *by George Coggeshall*—The Recollections of an American Schooner Captain.

TWILIGHT OF EMPIRE *by Sir Thomas Ussher & Sir George Cockburn*—Two accounts of Napoleon's Journeys in Exile to Elba and St. Helena: Narrative of Events by Sir Thomas Ussher & Napoleon's Last Voyage: Extract of a diary by Sir George Cockburn.

LEONAUR

ALSO FROM LEONAUR
AVAILABLE IN SOFTCOVER OR HARDCOVER WITH DUST JACKET

FARAWAY CAMPAIGN *by F. James*—Experiences of an Indian Army Cavalry Officer in Persia & Russia During the Great War.

REVOLT IN THE DESERT *by T. E. Lawrence*—An account of the experiences of one remarkable British officer's war from his own perspective.

MACHINE-GUN SQUADRON *by A. M. G.*—The 20th Machine Gunners from British Yeomanry Regiments in the Middle East Campaign of the First World War.

A GUNNER'S CRUSADE *by Antony Bluett*—The Campaign in the Desert, Palestine & Syria as Experienced by the Honourable Artillery Company During the Great War .

DESPATCH RIDER *by W. H. L. Watson*—The Experiences of a British Army Motorcycle Despatch Rider During the Opening Battles of the Great War in Europe.

TIGERS ALONG THE TIGRIS *by E. J. Thompson*—The Leicestershire Regiment in Mesopotamia During the First World War.

HEARTS & DRAGONS *by Charles R. M. F. Crutwell*—The 4th Royal Berkshire Regiment in France and Italy During the Great War, 1914-1918.

INFANTRY BRIGADE: 1914 *by John Ward*—The Diary of a Commander of the 15th Infantry Brigade, 5th Division, British Army, During the Retreat from Mons.

DOING OUR 'BIT' *by Ian Hay*—Two Classic Accounts of the Men of Kitchener's 'New Army' During the Great War including *The First 100,000* & *All In It*.

AN EYE IN THE STORM *by Arthur Ruhl*—An American War Correspondent's Experiences of the First World War from the Western Front to Gallipoli-and Beyond.

STAND & FALL *by Joe Cassells*—With the Middlesex Regiment Against the Bolsheviks 1918-19.

RIFLEMAN MACGILL'S WAR *by Patrick MacGill*—A Soldier of the London Irish During the Great War in Europe including *The Amateur Army*, *The Red Horizon* & *The Great Push*.

WITH THE GUNS *by C. A. Rose & Hugh Dalton*—Two First Hand Accounts of British Gunners at War in Europe During World War 1- Three Years in France with the Guns and With the British Guns in Italy.

THE BUSH WAR DOCTOR *by Robert V. Dolbey*—The Experiences of a British Army Doctor During the East African Campaign of the First World War.